JAMES KERR-LAWSON
A CANADIAN ABROAD

"Why should we require a dramatic or
moral peg to hang beautiful painting
upon . . . The fact is it doesn't require
it, and is much better without it . . . "

Letter to Homer Watson, December, 1889

ART GALLERY OF WINDSOR   1983

80   Portrait of Homer Watson   ca. 1930s

FOREWORD

The genesis of this exhibition dates from July 29, 1978, when the Art Gallery of Windsor acquired at auction, in Birmingham, Michigan, the painting *"Music, when soft voices die, Vibrates in the memory"* (cat. no. 3). James Kerr-Lawson was twenty-three years old when he painted this graceful study of two daughters of the mayor of Hamilton, Ontario, in 1885.

In July, 1978, we knew little about the artist but we did know that the painting was a work of considerable sensitivity and skill. So, with the donors' help, we repatriated it.

Shortly thereafter, we learned that Robert Lamb, then at Carleton University, Ottawa, had been doing research on James Kerr-Lawson and that he would be interested in working with us on an exhibition of the artist's work. We engaged him to do it.

As a result of his efforts during the past few years, we now know a great deal about James Kerr-Lawson, his studies in Toronto and abroad, his life as an expatriate Canadian, his associations with distinguished men and women in the arts and letters in Great Britain, continental Europe and Canada in the years before and after the turn of the century.

The purpose of this first survey exhibition is to share that knowledge with students and with the Canadian public; to introduce the work of an accomplished Canadian about which virtually nothing has been seen or known.

I am indebted to many of the artist's relatives, most notably Miss Norah McCullough of Guelph, Ontario, to the descendants of some of Kerr-Lawson's friends and patrons in England and Wales, and to all the other institutions and individuals who have freely shared their knowledge and, in most cases, their prized pictures for the extended tour of this collection.

I am also grateful to Ted Fraser, curator, who initiated the project with Mr. Lamb and will be in charge of its travels across Canada, to Betty Wilkinson, registrar, whose work in editing all of the catalogue materials and watching over all of the technical details of this publication has been meticulous, to Ken Ferguson, business manager, Erika Schafer, secretary, Ron Lauzon and Marty Hunt, preparators, for devoting many hours of time in helping to bring the exhibition into being and preparing it for travel in Canada. The Fine Art Society Limited, London, England, has been exceedingly generous in co-ordinating and arranging for the shipment of loans of paintings from the United Kingdom.

The contribution of Robert Lamb, University of Manitoba, in selecting works for the exhibition and writing the catalogue, has been the major one. On behalf of all who view the exhibition and, more importantly, make use of this publication in years to come, I should like to express my thanks. Mr. Lamb has worked hard for a very long time, has been patient in accepting our criticisms and suggestions and could hardly have been more co-operative or cheerful in seeing the project through.

The Ontario Arts Council and The Canada Council provided initial financial assistance to get the project underway, The Museum Assistance Programme of National Museums of Canada has provided the major funding required to bring James Kerr-Lawson, through his pictures, back to Canada. My thanks to all of them. To the artist, welcome back. It's been a long time!

Kenneth Saltmarche
Director
Art Gallery of Windsor
September 29, 1982

ITINERARY

Macdonald Stewart Art Centre, Guelph, Ont.
February 12 to March 20, 1983

Burnaby Art Gallery, Burnaby, B.C.
September 21 to October 23, 1983

Art Gallery of Windsor, Windsor, Ont.
April 10 to May 22, 1983

Glenbow Museum, Calgary, Alberta
November 11 to December 18, 1983

Art Gallery of Ontario, Toronto, Ont.
June 4 to August 14, 1983

Beaverbrook Art Gallery, Fredericton, N.B.
January 15 to February 15, 1984

ACKNOWLEDGMENTS

Three and a half years of research have enabled me to bring together, for this exhibition and its catalogue, a great deal of previously unknown or uncollected information about James Kerr-Lawson. Some sources, however, could not be properly tapped, especially English, Scottish and Italian newspapers and magazines. I will be grateful to anyone who may have further information about Kerr-Lawson's works or life than is mentioned in the catalogue and is willing to share such information with me.

There are many sources, however, which have been opened to me and many people whom I should like to thank. Myron Laskin, Jr., of the National Gallery of Canada, first brought to my attention the Art Gallery of Windsor's plans for a Kerr-Lawson exhibition. Several members of the artist's family have been especially helpful. Miss Norah McCullough, his niece, has been an invaluable contact and source of good advice and Mrs. Peter F. Groff has sent me the relevant sections of the Lawson family archives.

The staffs of many museums, archives and libraries have gone out of their way to find obscure pieces of information for me. Maija Vilcins, Charles C. Hill, Michael Pantazzi and Alan McNairn, all of the National Gallery of Canada, deserve special thanks for this.

Others who have helped beyond the call of duty are Sir Harold Acton, Janet Braide, Clifford M. Brown, T. Ladd Hilland, Roger Mortimer, Joan Murray, Hugh Stevenson and Linda Street.

I appreciate the opportunity provided by the Art Gallery of Windsor to play a part in bringing to wide public attention the work of this accomplished and little-known Canadian artist.

Thank you all for everything you have done.

R. J. L.

45 *Florence, Showing the Bridges Spanning the Arno*   *[undated]*
Reproduced by Gracious Permission of Her Majesty The Queen

Her Majesty Queen Elizabeth II

Mr. K. Y. Alghanim, Windsor, England

The Hon. Charles Allsopp, London, England

Art Gallery of Ontario, Toronto

Art Gallery of Windsor, Ontario

Beaverbrook Art Gallery, Fredericton, New Brunswick

Chelsea Library, The Royal Borough of Kensington & Chelsea, London, England

City of Kingston upon Hull, Museums and Art Galleries, Hull, England

The Fine Art Society Limited, London, England

Mr. Derek FitzGerald, London, England

The Fitzwilliam Museum, Cambridge

The FORBES Magazine Collection, New York City

Roger Gibbs, Esq., London, England

Mrs. Peter F. Groff, Andover, Massachusetts

Mrs. Barbara Halpern, Oxford, England

Mr. B. Peter Hennessy, Vancouver, British Columbia

Dr. Douglas Kerr-Lawson, Waterloo, Ontario

Mr. Thomas P. Kohn-Speyer, Hailsham, East Sussex

Leslie Maddock Lash, White Plains, New York

Mr. and Mrs. Jules Loeb, Toronto, Ontario

Mrs. John McConville, London, England

Dr. Dorothy J. McCullough, Toronto, Ontario

Dr. J. A. L. McCullough, McMurray, Pennsylvania

Miss Norah McCullough, Guelph, Ontario

The National Gallery of Canada, Ottawa

National Portrait Gallery, London

Mr. and Mrs. Edmund Paul Speyer, Tenby, South Wales

Mrs. Keith Thomson, North Vancouver, British Columbia

University Art Museum, University of California, Berkeley

University of Guelph Collection/Macdonald Stewart Art Centre, Guelph, Ontario

and private lenders

TABLE OF CONTENTS

37 St. Paul's Cathedral, London ca. 1906-11

JAMES KERR-LAWSON: A SHORT CHRONOLOGY

1862	Born in Scotland, 28 October.
ca. 1866	Family emigrated to Hamilton, Ontario.
1879-80	Attended Ontario School of Art, Toronto.
1880-81	In Rome with Luigi Galli, and at Accademia di Belle Arte and Académie de France.
1881-84	At Académie Julian, Paris.
ca. 1883	Befriended by William Brymner.
1884	With Brymner and F. W. Jackson at Runswick Bay, Yorkshire. In November, returned to Canada.
1885-87	In Ottawa, Toronto and Hamilton. Elected A.R.C.A. and O.S.A. Spent summers with Homer Watson. Met Catherine Adah Muir.
1887	Return to Europe. Study in Paris and Rome.
1888	In Pittenweem, Fifeshire. Joined by Watsons, Smiths and Cassy Muir. Departed for Tangier.
1889	Return from Tangier. Marriage to Cassy Muir, 24 September. Autumn and winter in Pittenweem.
1890-98	Exhibited with Royal Glasgow Institute of Fine Arts.
1891-94	In Kirkintilloch, Dunbartonshire, with winters in Tangier. Befriended by Whistler and George Frederick Watts.
1893-94	Worked in Spain.
1894	Painted Verlaine in Paris. Took up seasonal residence in Florence.
1894-98	Resided in Glasgow at times. Often in ill-health.
1898	Exhibited with International Society of Sculptors, Painters and Gravers in London.
1899	Set up by Berenson as art dealer.
1900	Moved to Glebe Place, Chelsea.
1901	Founding member of Society of Painters in Tempera.
1903	One-man show at Dowdeswell Galleries. Began Stoke Rochford Hall murals and first of several magazine articles.
1906	Stoke Rochford murals exhibited at Alpine Club Gallery, London. Aldenham House murals commissioned.
1908	Publication of "The Influence of the Franciscan Legend on Italian Art." Founding member of Senefelder Club.
1912-15	Exhibited with Canadian Art Club, Toronto.
1913-15	Designed London Transport posters.
1914	One-man show at Twenty-One Gallery, London.
1916	Contributed lithograph to Red Cross war benefit. Caterina (Cassy) worked in nurses' hostel.
1917-18	Painted Arras and Ypres for Canadian War Memorials.
1922	With Frank Brangwyn, organized British section of Venice Biennale. Studio visited by Queen Mary.
1924	Designed paper mosaics for chapel of British Empire Exhibition.
1926	Exhibited at Beaux Arts Gallery, London.
1930	Exhibited at Beaux Arts Gallery, London.
1939	Died in London, 1 May.

A CANADIAN ABROAD

James Kerr-Lawson is a little known Canadian painter who once had and now deserves a much larger reputation. His works, at their best, are handsomely composed, pure in colour, refined in technique and often witty in conception. At first he was a Realist but eventually he became a decorative painter, strongly influenced by Renaissance art. On a formal or philosophical level he is not a James Wilson Morrice or Ozias Leduc. His work, however, compares well with that of his Canadian contemporaries: Horatio Walker, George Reid, Homer Watson, William Brymner or Paul Peel.

On a historical level, Kerr-Lawson is of the greatest interest. He was not an influential teacher, propagandist or builder of cultural institutions. He was, instead, an expatriate, pursuing his own muse in an international context. His reputation too was international, and his contacts were important and progressive ones for his time. In Canada he was close both to Homer Watson and William Brymner and was a member of the Canadian Art Club. Abroad he was close to such figures as George Frederick Watts, James McNeill Whistler, and Bernard Berenson, to such groups as the Glasgow School and International Society and to such movements as the mural painting and lithography revivals. Of his Canadian contemporaries, probably only Morrice and Walker had more important contacts and larger international reputations. By 1908, Kerr-Lawson was seen as one of those Canadian painters who held

> positions of respect and honour among the world's great painters . . . [who] brought honour to their native land and renown to themselves.[1]

Kerr-Lawson's reputation and contacts, however, were of a type that has not fared well historically. First, he was an expatriate four times over, with a reputation broadly but thinly based. Thus he is a figure very little known, in whom nationalists have had little vested interest. Second, his contacts were British and now are of less artistic prestige than French ones. For the artists of Kerr-Lawson's generation, however, expatriation, cosmopolitanism and British contacts were considered very desirable.

During the last half of the nineteenth century, British power and influence in Canada were at their height. France might be pre-eminent in painting but Britain had a broader and deeper cultural influence. Among the English

speaking upper and middle classes, there was pride in Britain's power and in Canada's place as the most progressive nation within the Empire, an empire that could allow full scope to their highest human ambitions. The importance of this imperialist tradition has been established by historians like Carl Berger[2]. Even among basically apolitical artists, it operated on several levels. British painters like John Fraser, Lucius O'Brien and Frederic Marlett Bell-Smith were the backbone of Canadian artists' societies and, naturally, brought their British opinions with them. British musicians dominated Canadian music and British writers and scholars were equally active. Canadians also were trained in Britain and some-times continued their careers there. Painters like Kerr-Lawson, Mary Bell Eastlake and Elizabeth A. Forbes all chose to live in Britain. The same was true for writers like Sir Gilbert Parker, Lily Dougall and Grant Allen. Steven Leacock remained in Canada but was still a fervent anglophile and imperialist. Many Canadian musicians such as Emma Albani, Louise Edvina, Harry Field and Nora Clench based themselves in London. While British influence has declined since World War I, it still provided a strong foundation for the work of the Group of Seven and for writers like Hugh MacLennan. British musicians like Healey Willan and Sir Ernest MacMillan dominated Canadian music into the 1950s. British ties in business and politics were maintained equally late by figures like Lord Beaverbrook and Vincent Massey.

Kerr-Lawson is an important painter within this British tradition. His works can be very fine and he is of great historical interest. It is hoped he will now obtain the reputation he deserves.

James Kerr-Lawson was born on October 28, 1862 in Cellardyke (now part of Anstruther), an ancient prawn-fishing port on the south coast of Fifeshire, Scotland. He was the second child of William Lawson and Jessie Kerr. William Lawson (1830-1913) was a ship's carpenter and boatbuilder from an old Fifeshire seafaring family. Jessie Kerr (1838-1917) had more obscure origins. Her parentage is uncertain but she was raised by a couple called Kerr, in the village of St. Monance, near Anstruther. They

1. D. R. Wilkie, President of the Canadian Art Club, in the *Toronto World,* 4 February 1908.

2. Carl Berger, *The Sense of Power,* University of Toronto Press: Toronto, 1970. See also articles listed in the bibliography by Douglas Cole, Terry Cook and Robert J. D. Page.

managed to have her educated as a teacher in Edinburgh and, on May 30, 1860, she married William Lawson in the Church of Scotland in St. Monance. Fourteen months later, Andrew Cowper, their first son was born. Fifteen months thereafter came James Kerr and then a succession of three sons and five daughters.[3] In 1865, after a shipwreck and exposure, William Lawson suffered from heart and hearing problems that within eight years would make him an invalid and throw the burden of supporting the family onto Jessie. In 1866, she persuaded him to emigrate to Canada, where he settled in Hamilton, Ontario and, for several years, worked as a carpenter in a shipyard. By 1869, the family was listed in directories as living at 247 James Street North. Jessie was already contributing to the family income through a small business in dry goods and millinery. She would gradually turn her literary talents to journalism, become a columnist for several newspapers, write four novels and books of verse and become a well known figure in her field. Even today, her name appears in dictionaries of Canadian biography.[4] She was a loving mother but also a driving perfectionist with a passion for education she communicated to her children.

Fig. 1   James as a boy in Hamilton

Kerr-Lawson and his brothers and sisters attended the Hamilton Public Grammar School and then the Collegiate Institute, where James took the classical curriculum under George Dickson, later Headmaster of Upper Canada College. He and Andrew were very bright and James already showed great artistic promise. Dickson encouraged the brothers' ambitions and when James's education was threatened by precarious family finances, it was Dickson who helped to support him. This was in 1879, when Kerr-Lawson went to Toronto to the recently formed Ontario School of Art. Here he studied under the landscape painter Thomas Mower Martin and may well have been exposed to the influence of Robert Harris, the young Realist painter recently back from Paris. None of his student works have come to light to show a possible Harris influence, though the earliest known works, from several years later, show similar directness, careful lighting and composition, dark colour tonalities and loose, broad paint application.

In April 1880, Kerr-Lawson won the School's first prize in elementary freehand drawing[5] and decided to study further in Europe. His strong classical bent led him first to Rome, where he studied briefly at the Académie de France in the Villa Medici and at the Accademia di Belle Arte. He learned more from frequenting such artists' rendezvous as the Caffè Greco on the Via Condotti. It was there he met his first serious master, the painter Luigi Galli (1820-1900). How Galli influenced him is uncertain. It was probably not through his own symbolic paintings, with their bravura brushwork but through his enthusiasm for Venetian art and for the works of George Frederick Watts. Both Watts and the Venetians would play a major part in Kerr-Lawson's later life.

He did not stay long in Rome but travelled south to Naples and Capri and soon sent home paintings to the 1882 and 1883 exhibitions of the Royal Canadian Academy and Art Association of Montreal. These paintings are now unlocated but are mentioned in newspaper reviews. The critic for *The Witness* wrote:

> Mr. Lawson, another self-made Canadian artist, has three very ambitious and poetic southern Italian pieces. They are in that unfinished condition that draws much upon the imagination. The cactus bower is a very happy conception, and the twilight hillside with a goat wandering upon it is very suggestive of Capri or the goat island, where it is said to have been painted.[6]

The critic for *The Globe* described *The Cactus Bower, Capri* as:

> a tropical scene in which the breadth of colouring aptly presents the flood of sunlight. A bit of intensely blue sky is visible and the intermingling of dark patches of shadow and gleams of sunlight under the cool, broad cactus leaves is admirably done. A female figure, with pose and features expressive of langour and negligence is in keeping with the scene.[7]

He was displeased by the lack of atmospheric clarity in *A*

3. William and Jessie Lawson's children were Andrew Cowper, James Kerr, Katharine Leslie, Elizabeth McKenzie, Alice-Margaret, William Leslie, Anstruther Abercrombie, Edward Kerr, Jessie Kerr and Jean.

4. *Macmillan Dictionary of Canadian Biography*, 4th edition, 1978, p. 449.

5. Ontario Society of Artists, Minute Book, 22 April 1880.

6. "The Art Gallery," *The Witness* (Montreal), 11 April 1883.

7. "The Art Exhibition," *The Globe* (Toronto), 26 May 1883.

1 *Portrait of Alice Margaret Lawson   ca. 1882-83*

Capri Landscape but concluded that this was probably the artist's intention. He had similarly mixed feelings toward *Winnowing,* a scene of a peasant girl working in the fields at twilight. "The figure is boldly drawn," he wrote, "and the action natural, but the peculiar effects of the school in the description of the surroundings do not set off the subject to advantage."[8] These comments suggest that the reviewers were probably older artists trained in a tradition of precise detail and suspicious of the broader Realist style in which Kerr-Lawson was working. Mention of pastoral and peasant subjects and of effects of light suggest that he must have been working in a Barbizon School style.

By the fall of 1881, Kerr-Lawson was in Paris, at the Académie Julian, studying under the classical genre painter Gustave Boulanger and the portraitist Jules-Joseph Lefebvre. What he learned there was not so much a part of the curriculum as part of the artistic milieu of the city. By the late 1870s, a modified form of Realism, shorn of radical politics, had been absorbed into the academies. In 1882, Courbet was finally accorded a retrospective at the Ecole des Beaux Arts. A second generation of Realists, somewhat influenced by Impressionism, was also emerging, led by the figure of Jules Bastien-Lepage whose *Joan of Arc* and *Beggar,* in the 1880 and 1881 Salons, were attracting many imitators.[9] Bastien's was an acceptable, consensus style, based more on the naturalism of Degas than the prismatic colourism of Monet. With Bastien and his followers there was a loosening of brushwork, lightening of palette and direct observation of non-ideal subjects. Unlike Monet, however, they maintained an interest in significant subject matter, in tightly structured compositions and in relatively high finish, in which form never dissolved in space. Another painter then attracting followers was the American expatriate James McNeill Whistler, whose portraits of his mother, of Thomas Carlyle and Cicely Alexander created a strong impression at the Salons of 1883 and 1884. Whistler's work sprang from similar roots in Degas, Velasquez and *Japonisme.* His painting style was broader but he too was concerned with balanced compositions and subtle, low tonalities, raised to an exquisite pitch. Realist subject matter he abhorred. The eighties and nineties would see a Realist-Impressionist style spread around the world and then be abandoned by the turn of the century avant-garde. It would be in this style that Kerr-Lawson would come to prominence.

Little is known of Kerr-Lawson's first two years in Paris. On November 20, 1881, on a visit to the city, Robert Harris mentioned seeing him.[10] On December 5, William Blair Bruce, a fellow Hamiltonian at the Académie Julian, commented in a letter, "Have seen nothing of Lawson as yet and am not particularly anxious about it."[11] A Bruce letter, from December 11, 1883, indicates that Kerr-Lawson visited home to see his family[12] but further letters indicate that he was back in Paris by January 1884.

By then Kerr-Lawson was friendly with the Canadian painter William Brymner and with the Englishman Frederick William Jackson. Writing to his father, on March 4, Brymner mentioned:

> I have been talking this evening to Jackson and Lawson about where we will go this summer and we have almost come to the conclusion that Yorkshire would be a better place than Belgium. My objection was on the ground of its being dearer, but from a liberal calculation they made based on several years experience of Jackson, we can live for from fifteen to twenty shillings a week if three or four go together.[13]

From Brymner's and Bruce's later comments, it appears that Kerr-Lawson was a charming but feckless boy, who still had to find some direction. On April 6, Brymner noted:

> Lawson is twenty-two nearly, and if he had the good fortune to possess five francs would spend it all in offering you cigars and coffee, even if he didn't expect to have any more money till the end of the month, never thinking of how he would manage to put in the intervening fifteen days. Reckless in what he says, does and spends but the sort of boy you can't help liking. He'll spend any amount of trouble on a piece of work and nearly finish it. The next time you see him he will as likely as not have given it away to someone who happened to fancy it. There's any amount of stuff in him of the right sort if we can get him to settle down to work. He has plenty of ideas in the way of pictures and compositions but has not quite enough patience.[14]

More snobbishly, Blair Bruce recalled:

> I saw young Lawson in Paris one evening, at the Café des Ecoles, a place I would only care about going once a year. The crowd are too skinny. He's a nice boy, apparently not much force of character yet, but guess he'll sprout.[15]

The works Kerr-Lawson finished in Paris have by now largely disappeared. In 1883-84, however, he painted a dark, direct, broadly worked portrait of the aged Victor Hugo (Collection Mme. G. R. Varin, Versailles). It is said to have been painted from life but this cannot be proved. Brymner also mentioned two landscapes:

> one from Tennyson's Goose and the Golden Eggs, (An old man standing at an old broken down cottage door, with an old woman in a like condition, standing at it, receiving a goose from his arms. The wind blowing everything and pools of water in the muddy road.) the other Maud Muller.[16]

8. Ibid.

9. On second generation Realism see Gabriel P. Weisberg, *The Realist Tradition* and on Bastien-Lepage see Kenneth McConkey, "The Bouguereau of the Naturalists: Bastien-Lepage and British Art," *Art History,* 1978, pp. 371-82.

10. Harris to his father, 20 November 1881, Harris Papers, National Gallery of Canada, Ottawa.

11. Bruce to his father, 5 December 1881, Bruce Papers, Art Gallery of Hamilton, Hamilton.

12. Ibid., 11 December 1883.

13. Brymner to his father, 4 March 1884, Brymner Papers, McCord Museum, Montreal.

14. Ibid., 6 April 1884.

15. Bruce to his father, 9 April 1884, Bruce Papers.

16. Brymner to his father, 6 April 1884, Brymner Papers.

While the Hugo portrait is painted in a conservative Realist manner, the two landscapes were probably in a plein-air style like that of Brymner or Bastien-Lepage. Their use of literary sources would also be consistent with the Bastien influence.

After a trip to Brolles, in the forest of Fontainebleau, in April 1884, Brymner, Jackson and Kerr-Lawson returned to Paris. On the thirtieth they went to the Salon and the next day left for Runswick Bay, Yorkshire, where they planned to spend the summer. As they had little money, they bypassed London and were soon in the tiny North Sea fishing village. They boarded at the Sheffield Hotel, grew beards, sketched on the docks and soon were bored with the quietness of the place. They continued on through November, with few amusements except quoits and an occasional visitor. One "knew all about the smaller villages about Naples and Capri and knew people Lawson knew there".[17] Brymner was very productive, painting among other things, his famous *A Wreath of Flowers* (National Gallery of Canada). Kerr-Lawson exhibited a painting of the village green in Runswick at the 1885 Royal Canadian Academy exhibition but otherwise, according to Brymner, had "not managed to get anything worth speaking of finished this summer. He carries things on to a certain distance in the most clever way possible, but then he gets disgusted and leaves off so that the result is not money."[18] In late November, the trio split up and Kerr-Lawson sailed from Liverpool on the twenty-seventh. He was to have taken a number of Brymner paintings with him but, confusing his schedule and thus having to leave earlier than expected, he was not able to do so. "As Lawson is the most careless fellow on earth, perhaps it is just as well . . ." commented Brymner.[19]

In Canada, Kerr-Lawson stayed with his brother Andrew, who was working in Ottawa for the Geological Survey, and later with his family, in Toronto, where they had moved in 1881. He suddenly became very active. During his first year, he showed twelve oils and three watercolours with the Royal Canadian Academy, Ontario Society of Artists and Art Association of Montreal. On May fifteenth and November third respectively, he was elected to the first two societies. Soon he exhibited one of his finest works, *Music, when soft voices die, Vibrates in the memory* (cat. no. 3) at the O.S.A. Winter Exhibition. With its poetic title taken from Shelley, *Music . . .* might well have been a conventional, Pre-Raphaelite work, yet in composition is strikingly reminiscent of Whistler's famous painting of 1858-59, *At the Piano* (Taft Museum, Cincinnati, Ohio).[20] This is probably just a coincidence. *At the Piano*

was not well known until the late nineties. *Music . . .*, also, is far more concerned with effects of light than *At the Piano,* with subtle, silver grey tones. These could well have come from Whistler's later works or from works of Bastien-Lepage.

Through Toronto art circles, Kerr-Lawson now got to know the painter Homer Watson, who became a lifelong friend. For several summers they worked together at Watson's home in Doon. He also grew close to Miss Catherine Adah Muir.[21] Cassy (later known as Caterina) was a bright, vivacious, dominating personality, who would play a major role in forwarding Kerr-Lawson's career.

About this time he painted her portrait (cat. no. 6). In style it is a typical early work and one of the finest he ever did. It is a life size, full-length profile view of her in a white silk ball gown. She is turned to the right and posed against a dark, green-brown damask ground. With her pointed nose and prominent chin, Cassy is not beautiful but, with the contrasts between the ground, her hair, skin and gown, she makes a striking figure. This is the essence of the portrait. It is based on Cassy's physical presence, especially the tonal contrasts and gradations on her gown and her placement within the frame. Its profile pose prevents much psychological penetration. Its physical directness of approach places it well within the Realist tradition yet its formal concern with tone and composition, coming from Whistler or Bastien-Lepage, foreshadows much of the decorative tendency in Kerr-Lawson's later works.

During 1886, he was busy with landscape and genre painting and also occasional portraits. Besides his family, he portrayed James Smith of the R.C.A. (cat. no. 4) and the Rev. Henry James Grasett, Dean of St. James' Cathedral. His works now attracted notice. The critic for the *Ottawa Citizen* mentioned *Music* and its "tenderness of tone" and described the subject of *The Orphans* as "three children at a table taking a scanty meal; a dog looks up".[22] The *Montreal Herald,* later that year, described his painting, *Hoeing Potatoes,* as showing an old woman and boy at work in the fields.[23] A more critical view of him at this time is contained in a letter from the dealer, James Spooner, to his friend Homer Watson. Spooner was at the Imperial and Colonial Exhibition, in London (where Brymner's *Wreath of Flowers* was on display), and wrote back to Watson:

What you tell me about Mr. Lawson is excellent. Not much poesy in him and, although I have always thought him on the

17. Ibid., 28 May 1884. "Maud Muller" was a poem by John Greenleaf Whittier.

18. Ibid., 28 November 1884.   19. Ibid.

20. A history of *At the Piano* is given by Andrew MacLaren Young, *Paintings of James McNeill Whistler* (New Haven: Yale University Press, 1980), vol. 1, no. 24, pp. 8-9.

21. Cassy Muir was born in Scarborough, Ontario, on 18 November 1860. She was the daughter of John and Eliza Muir. She was raised by her maternal grandmother in Hamilton and may have known the Lawsons through membership in the Central Presbyterian Church. During the early 1870s, Eliza Muir married David Allan Smith and produced four children: Frances, Elizabeth, Adah and William. Widowed in 1884, she and all her children accompanied the Watsons to Europe in 1887. They lived with Kerr-Lawson for several years and all later eventually lived in Torquay, Devonshire.

22. "Royal Academy Exhibition," *Ottawa Citizen,* 3 February 1886.

23. "Original Drawings," *Montreal Herald,* — October 1886.

right track, he *must* go further. He does indeed see good colour but that is not enough. Let him lay in groundwork and build and beautify. This he must do before he can be considered beyond rudiments ... Let Mr. Lawson work and certain qualities will likely be exhibited by him. But he is not there yet.[24]

A more generous appreciation came in March 1887, in an article in *The Week*. Reviewing the opening of a new Toronto gallery, the Rembrandt Art Rooms, the writer commented:

Chiefest, perhaps, among the attractions of the "Rembrandt" easels just now, is a picture by Mr. James Kerr-Lawson of Hamilton. Nor will any one who is familiar with Mr. Lawson's work be surprised to find a canvas of his dominating a room full of pictures, many the work of older and better known men than he ... The present picture marks something of a departure from Mr. Lawson's usual manner and choice of subject ... We have always looked to him for truth and energy and genius of interpretation ... but he has not always or often given us the grace, the tenderness, the gentle, natural beautiful sentiment of his last picture. It is a girl at a piano. She is leaning forward, her face upon the music, her elbows upon the keys and her hand, in the first quick gesture of grief indulged, pressing her tear-filled eyes ... The girl is in an evening dress of white brocade, the arrangement and texture of which strike one ... as being particularly good. It is a triumph of the artist.[25]

The painting in question is now unlocated though it probably relates closely both to *Music* ... and to her portrait of Cassy (cat. no. 6) in a very similar dress. The degree to which the writer sentimentalizes its subject can only be suspected. The critic from *The Week* returned to the Rembrandt Art Rooms in October of the same year to notice that Kerr-Lawson was showing:

a fine study of a head, painted in the best manner of the French school—alive, human, startlingly real and naturally rendered, especially the nose, the hair on the forehead, the relentless truth of the ugly colouring.[26]

By the time of this second notice, however, Kerr-Lawson had become discouraged with his prospects in Toronto and had gone abroad. He, the Watsons, the Smiths and Cassy Muir all left for Europe during the summer. The Watsons settled near London and the Smiths somewhere in France while Kerr-Lawson studied in Paris. During the spring of 1888 he was in Rome, where he painted a small watercolour of a man with a pick, now in the Edmonton Art Gallery.

By early summer James was back in Britain, reunited with his mother and brother Andrew, who were then visiting the country. At their suggestion, in order to reduce expenses, he decided to go to Pittenweem, a Fifeshire fishing village near Anstruther. In July he was joined there by the Watsons, the Smiths and Cassy.

From their rented rooms, they ventured forth to paint and explore the countryside. In the evening, they sat and talked. They greatly enjoyed each other's company and both Kerr-Lawson and Watson completed a lot of work. In late September James left to paint in Tangier, Morocco, a popular winter painting place for European artists as it was easy to get to, abounded in exotic Oriental motifs and was not yet overrun by tourists. He and Cassy would return to Tangier many times and Moroccan subjects would come to be an important part of his oeuvre. At one point he even imported a Moroccan servant to work for him in London. Little is known of his first stay in Morocco except that he took a trip into the interior to hunt wild boar, and, by the spring of 1889, sent eight Moroccan paintings to the O.S.A. and R.C.A. exhibitions. One of these is probably the small seascape, *Mediterranean Coast, Morocco* (cat. no. 9).

In the meantime, everyone else continued on at Pittenweem. Cassy and Roxa Watson were busy learning French and promoting Homer's works to anyone who would listen. "I tell you," Roxa wrote, "Cassy is the one to have with a person to sell pictures. She lays it on thick, I can tell you. She does not say anything more than she believes ..."[27] This comment would be repeated again and again to the end of Cassy's life. Much of her husband's subsequent reputation would depend on her selling ability.

Homer Watson, however, was tiring of Pittenweem and yearning to get back to London. He had had works accepted at the Glasgow Institute of Fine Arts and Royal Society of British Artists (Whistler was then their president), and it was probably following his example that Kerr-Lawson sent his works to these societies starting in 1890.

In May 1889, everyone left Pittenweem, visited the Paris Salon and then came to London for the annual Royal Academy exhibition and other shows. The Smiths probably summered in Germany but the Watsons retired to Maidenhead, just west of London, where they stayed with relatives, the Biggses, and then got a cottage of their own. Homer revived his friendship with George Clausen, who was then living nearby, and was soon learning etching under his direction. It was also probably through Watson that Clausen and Kerr-Lawson soon became friends.

Kerr-Lawson returned from Morocco in late August and by then was engaged to Cassy Muir. By early

24. Spooner to Watson, 23 July 1886, Watson Papers, National Gallery of Canada, Ottawa.

25. "Art: Mr. Lawson's New Picture," *The Week* (Toronto), 17 March 1887, p. 257.

26. "Rembrandt House," *The Week*, 20 October 1887, p. 760.

27. Roxa to Phoebe Watson, 10 February 1889, in Frank E. Page, *Homer Watson*, p. 144.

9   *Mediterranean Coast, Morocco   1888*

74   *Unknown Spanish Castle   [undated]*

September they were both in Maidenhead. "Jim Lawson looks some older," wrote Roxa Watson. "He wears a beard which improves him very much. I do not think . . . Cassy looks any older—she is always taken to be about twenty-one or two."[28] On September 24, they were married in the Register Office of the nearby village of Cookham with Homer Watson and Edward Biggs as witnesses. That afternoon they left for London and the next day took the train to Scotland. The Watsons were surprised that Cassy had consented to marry James. Phoebe (Homer Watson's sister) wrote: "I forgot to tell you what I meant by Lawson defying fate and marrying. The lines in his hand indicated that he never would get married same as mine; people over here seem to think that Miss Muir might have done better than marry him but every one to their own taste don't you think so."[29]

Back in Pittenweem, Kerr-Lawson enjoyed a period of great productivity. "From what we hear from Scotland," noted Roxa Watson, "everybody seems to be happy up there. Jim has already sent twenty-four small pictures to Canada and has ever so many more on the way. You see what marrying does for some people."[30] Unfortunately his productivity did not continue, for during November and December he contracted pneumonia and became very dispirited. He wrote to Watson in January.

> . . . I don't know what excuse to offer you for writing tonight. You have always been kind to me, always treated me as a man and a brother and the only return I make you is to write to you when the damnation Jim-Jams, or the Hump is upon me. I sent you a photo of the picture I sent to Glasgow which was quite as inconsiderate an action as this writing to you now. This picture is 60 x 40 inches and a very sorry affair. I painted it I hardly know why but I know I would not have done it if I had been rich. I have now on the easel a smaller picture of a very dismal subject but better painted than the potato gatherers. It is the interior of Millar's shop with an old cove making a little white coffin and a little girl standing by who, as she watches the operation, clasps her flaxen haired dolly to her breast where she dimly feels the first premonitory stirrings of the maternal instinct.
>
> Since this is the subject, which I feel calls for another apology, I declare, dear Watson, that the effort to throw an element of interest into my work has almost crushed the life out of me. Why should we require a dramatic or moral peg to hang beautiful painting upon . . . The fact is it doesn't require it, and is much better without it . . .
>
> Oh Watson, it is a sad dismal world in the winter in Scotland when one is hard up, and the pleasant letters that drop in now and then here and there only seem to heighten the feeling of isolation . . . Needless to say, my dear Homer, that the foregoing has a dyspeptic hue.[31]

Watson had sent him some of his recent etchings and Kerr-Lawson then expressed his enthusiasm for them. "I would like awfully," he wrote,

> to scratch a plate with you and still more would I enjoy the printing of one. In some of your future experiments, Watson, try something for the sake of line as much as possible on the principle that the white is as precious as the black, in that a dark accent here and there on a light ground can be very telling. Thunder! I want to say so much to you about the business. These fragmentary remarks are almost an impertinence. What is the price of copper?[32]

Kerr-Lawson became active as an etcher and lithographer after 1900 but this is the first mention of his interest in prints.

During the eighties, many British artists had taken up needle and crayon. Following the example of Whistler, they created a printmaking movement that lasted through the twenties. Few of Kerr-Lawson's early prints are known. A small etching of a middle-aged woman in a bonnet is owned by one of his nephews.[33] A colour print of the Temple of Vesta, in Rome, was bought by the Leeds City Art Gallery in 1893.

Little is known of Kerr-Lawson's activities during the next few years. In the spring of 1890, he and Watson worked together again in Pittenweem and, later that year, he was in Kirkcudbrightshire (in S.W. Scotland) where he made a fine pastel of a farm girl, *Poor Sue* (cat. no. 13). He wanted to travel again in Italy but whether he got there is uncertain.

He must have spent some time in London for he developed a strong friendship with George Frederick Watts, revered patriarch of British Victorian painters. Watts introduced him to his other friends and eventually lent him his London studio for a successful exhibition of his paintings.[34] This was probably in 1899 for, later that year, the magazine *Saturday Night* carried an interview in which Watts predicted Kerr-Lawson's success. "Shall J. Kerr-Lawson," it began,

> that young Canadian artist . . . of whom several magazines have said such kind things, really be successful as an artist finally, and make for himself a career? This was the question put this summer to Sir James Watt [sic], R.A., in his own home. "Yes, surely," was the answer of this authority, "he shall. He has two, at least, of the essential qualifications of a successful artist. He has a good wife and he has intellect."[35]

By 1891, Kerr-Lawson and the Smiths were renting Oxgang House, a large villa in Kirkintilloch, on the northeastern outskirts of Glasgow. Here they would stay for about three years. The only mention of them during

28. Roxa to Phoebe, 7 October 1889, Watson Papers.

29. Phoebe to Roxa, 3 December 1889.

30. Roxa to Phoebe, 30 October 1889.

31. Kerr-Lawson to Homer Watson, 11 January 1890, in Jane Van Every, *With Faith, Ignorance and Delight*, pp. 50-51 and Muriel Miller, *Homer Watson*, p. 39.

32. Ibid.

33. Dr. Douglas Kerr-Lawson, Waterloo.

34. Minutes of Canadian Art Club meeting, 1912, Kerr-Lawson clippings file, Art Gallery of Ontario Library, Toronto.

35. Jean Grant, "Studio and Gallery," *Saturday Night*, 30 December 1889, p. 9.

5 *Horse and Cart on Rural Road   November 1886*

these years is in a letter to Cassy, written years later by a Harry Swan, who had visited them at Oxgang House. Swan recalled:

> a flood of forgotten memories of . . . many pleasant visits to you in Kirkintilloch . . . of your husband and mother and two sisters and I think a small brother who was absorbed in model trains—of your going off to Morocco and returning with the results of that visit with paintings that warmed me to see in them the sun shining . . . of walks in your old walled garden with your husband in the moonlight.[36]

In moving to Kirkintilloch, Kerr-Lawson became part of the Glasgow School which, with the Newlyn School and New English Art Club, was then the rallying point for young British plein-air painters. Inspired by the Barbizon School, by Courbet, the Hague School, Bastien-Lepage, Whistler and the Impressionists, the "Glasgow Boys" (led by James Guthrie, W. Y. Macgregor, John Lavery, E. A. Hornell and George Henry) were painting their most important works and were a force in British art well into the Edwardian period. Lavery and Henry especially became Kerr-Lawson's longtime friends. He lived off and on in Glasgow itself from 1894 to 1898. He exhibited at the Royal Glasgow Institute of Fine Arts and was given his first one-man show at an unknown Glasgow gallery.[37] He

---

36. Swan to Caterina, 20 March 1947, Lawson family archives, Andover, Mass.

37. "Scottish Painter of Picturesque," *Glasgow Herald*, 22 February 1949.

also got his first mention in an important magazine, *The Magazine of Art,* which commented favourably on his Institute painting, *The Ploughman.*[38] Today he is little remembered in Glasgow.[39]

Besides Morocco, already mentioned, Kerr-Lawson spent much of the nineties in France, Spain and Italy. Many British artists were in Paris for the 1893 Salon and there he met Whistler, in his Rue de Bac studio, walked with him in the garden and discussed the sensation made by *The Buccaneers,* a painting by the young Frank Brangwyn.[40] When and how he joined Whistler's intimate circle is uncertain. It may have been through Watson, his Glasgow friends, or his brother Edward. Edward worked for Whistler's friend and publisher, William Heinemann. Heinemann was known for his dinner parties and it was probably through these that Kerr-Lawson became friendly with the potter and writer William De Morgan, the novelist Maurice Hewlett and the team of journalist-illustrators, Elizabeth and Joseph Pennell.

By June 1893, he was again in Tangier where he also became friendly with Frank Brangwyn. Years later he recalled their meeting in a portrait of Brangwyn (cat. no. 77). Writing of it, he said:

Many years ago, José Tapiro introduced me to Frank Brangwyn in Tangier. Brangwyn may not have worn the djellaba, as I did, but I have painted him now in the garb of a Moorish chief because that is how I seem to remember him, with all Morocco as his background: I mean the Morocco we reached by crossing from Tarifa to Tangier in a felucca, with a crew of smugglers carrying tobacco, Dutch gin, and guns to the Riff before the days when the Compagnie Générale Transatlantique had made that country safe enough for a Sunday-school treat![41]

For most of the next year he worked in Spain, especially in Madrid. Besides doing his own work, he helped his brother Edward compile a Heinemann guide-book to the Prado. He studied the Venetian masterworks there and copied some of them. A Maurice Hewlett letter refers to him "wrestling with the soul of Titian," probably over his copy of *The Entombment,* now lost.[42]

The two friends' enthusiasm for Venetian painting was part of a growing trend. It had been kindled by Ruskin's *Modern Painters* and *The Stones of Venice* and by Walter Pater's essay on "The School of Giorgione." It was developed in such scholarly works as Crowe and Cavalcaselle's *Life and Times of Titian* and Bernard Berenson's *Venetian Painters of the Renaissance.* It would influence many young artists of the day, especially those who were muralists.

Returning from Spain, Kerr-Lawson was in Paris during the late summer of 1894. William Heinemann, who was preparing an edition of the Goncourt journals, met him unexpectedly and commissioned a portrait of the Symbolist poet Paul Verlaine.

"Good God!" he exclaimed, "you are just the man I am looking for," and he packed me into a cab and drove to Blanchet in the rue Bonaparte, where I procured some material and we then rattled off to Verlaine's garret. Here, propped up by pillows, sat Verlaine, with his high cheek bones, sloping blue eyes, very wide nostrils, tangled yellow beard and a few wisps of blond hair. An atmosphere of charm seemed in the most unaccountable way to radiate from him, as he welcomed us in a soft, caressing voice. He talked and jested in peculiarly charming English, being well versed in Victorian literature, interspersing his conversation with quotations from Tennyson, De Quincey, Shelley and Keats.[43]

From the charcoal drawing made at this sitting (Collection of Mme. G. R. Varin, Versailles) an oil portrait (cat. no. 14) was painted which is now in the Fitzwilliam Museum in Cambridge. It is a direct, psychological portrait, less handsome and formal than Kerr-Lawson's other portraits and contrasting strongly with Eugene Carrière's visionary portrait of the poet.

The Kerr-Lawsons may have visited England that fall but by November they were in Florence, soon to be their second home. In settling there they followed in the footsteps of that earlier Canadian, Antoine-Sebastien Falardeau (1822-1889), famous in his day as a copyist of the old masters. On their arrival, they met Mrs. Janet Ross, writer and grand dame of the Anglo-Florentine colony. Mrs. Ross later remembered that:

In the late autumn two friends of 'Signor' [George Frederick Watts], Mr. and Mrs. Kerr-Lawson, came to Florence with a letter asking me to do all I could to help them. We at once liked both husband and wife, but as 'Signor' did not say what Mr. Kerr-Lawson's profession was, or what I was to do for them, I was rather puzzled. At last I asked him point-blank, rather I think to his surprise, as he thought 'Signor' had told me he was an artist. They settled at Settignano until they found a charming little nook, the old cottage that had once belonged to Boccaccio's father at Corbignano. We became very intimate, and Kerr-Lawson did an admirable portrait of Henry. [Henry James Ross, her husband, cat. no. 16.][44]

The Casa di Boccaccio, mentioned by Mrs. Ross, would be the Kerr-Lawson's home for over forty years. It was certainly larger than an "old cottage." The writer Edward Hutton, a friend and sometime resident there, described it as:

---

38. "The Chronicle of Art: Exhibitions," *The Magazine of Art,* April 1893, p. xxvii.

39. He is mentioned briefly in James Caw, *Scottish Painting Past and Present,* p. 389.

40. William de Belleroche, *Brangwyn's Pilgrimage,* p. 167.

41. "A Famous Royal Academician as a Moorish Chief: Mr. Frank Brangwyn," *The Illustrated London News,* 10 October 1931.

42. Hewlett to Kerr-Lawson, 14 December 1893, Lawson family archives.

43. James Kerr-Lawson, "A Newly 'Discovered' Portrait of Verlaine," *Apollo,* May 1939, p. 262.

44. Janet Ross, *The Fourth Generation,* p. 338.

14   Portrait of Paul Verlaine   ca. 1894

a house ... with two loggie half smothered in roses and a little shrine of the Madonna of the Swords. Casa di Boccaccio they call the place ... Perhaps by courtesy of the owner ... you will stay a little in the garden and see the beautiful courtyard with its old well and the ruined frescoes that may still be traced on the walls of what was once the tower, and the broken inscriptions.[45]

The Kerr-Lawsons soon had many friends in Florence. The most famous of them was their neighbour, the young American connoisseur of Renaissance art; Bernard Berenson. They met about 1897, through Janet Ross, and soon became intimate. By spring, Berenson and his wife, Mary, sat to Kerr-Lawson for small pencil portraits (Berenson Collection, Florence and the latter now unlocated). They were often back and forth between each other's villas and, when Berenson and Mary were formally married, in December 1900, Kerr-Lawson and Caterina were among the close friends present. As Berenson was growing rich, he liked to help his less fortunate friends.

Among the first to be helped were the Kerr-Lawsons, whose moneyless plight in their Fiesole villa had long worried Berenson. He put them on to paintings which could be picked up for a pittance; one, acquired in Venice for £15. went to a rich Glasgow merchant for £350. placing the Kerr-Lawsons, as Mary put it, 'three hundred and fifty pounds away from poverty'. Another, Mary learned, yielded an even more spectacular profit. Bought for £1., it sold for £900. Thus launched, Kerr-Lawson established himself as a private dealer, no longer dependent on the uncertain market for his own paintings.[46]

Kerr-Lawson was to be a dealer for the rest of his life.

During the late nineties the Kerr-Lawsons migrated with the seasons between Florence and Glasgow, with short spells in London. The best single record of their doings is in letters by Maurice Hewlett. In February 1897 he wrote to Kerr-Lawson, who again had been seriously ill with pneumonia, this time in Dumfries.

Never did I know so clear a case of Providence politely, but firmly, announcing that a man of your qualities of Head and Heart—and I may add, Lungs—should not live in Scotland, when there is London panting for you.

I hope you won't disregard the hint which seems to me unequivocal. Your Canary Islands are all very well for canaries and your Dumfries may suit Carlyle with his gravedigger philosophy but London is the place for a man of sensibility—you are stimulated without being goaded, you are amused without debauchery. When I add that you would also secure the wonderful opportunity of daily study of the Old Masters and of my Head (I will throw in a bust and shoulders only to be seen beside the Farnese torso) and you will at once perceive that you are forward in your ways and blind to your obvious interests.[47]

Several years later Kerr-Lawson finally took the hint and did settle in the metropolis. By 1898 the two friends were discussing his illustrations for a new edition of Hewlett's *Earthwork Out of Tuscany*. It was published by Dent in 1899 and generated much correspondence. Most of this was business but there was friendly talk of their meeting in Italy during the spring and of the Hewletts' delight with Kerr-Lawson's recent portrait of their son, Cecco (Mrs. Dorothy G. Hewlett, Tauranga, New Zealand). When *Earthwork* ... was released, Hewlett would write, in his preface:

One thing is very plain; whatever may be said of my pictures Mr. Kerr-Lawson in his has brought the very breath of the places I, you and I love. I come jigging with my commentary at his heels, and am well content; for I know I shall have a chance of a hearing while he holds your eyes.[48]

In May 1898, Kerr-Lawson exhibited with the International Society of Sculptors, Painters and Gravers, at their first exhibition, in London. His atmospheric view of Venice (now unlocated, photo in Witt Library) was described in the press as a "characteristic work" of the Glasgow School.[49] The International Society, organized by John Lavery and presided over by Whistler, was one of the most advanced exhibiting groups of its day, important for forging links between English and French artists through showing works by Monet, Sisley, Rodin, Bonnard, Toulouse-Lautrec and Cézanne. Kerr-Lawson remained a member of the Society right through the 1920s. The only other Canadian member was James Wilson Morrice.

In February 1899, Whistler travelled to Rome for the wedding of William Heinemann. On his way back, he stopped in Florence, where he was hosted by the Kerr-Lawsons. They visited the famous Uffizi gallery of artists' self-portraits, where Whistler paid dramatic homage to Velasquez and was ignored by the museum administration.[50] After Whistler's death, attempts were made to obtain one of his self-portraits for the collection. They did not meet with success.

The Kerr-Lawsons abandoned Scotland for London about 1900. They found a home in the heart of artistic Chelsea, at 4 Turner Studios, Glebe Place. It would be their home for over fifty years. Glebe Place was a short street full of studios. During the nineties, it had seen such famous residents as Walter Sickert, William Rothenstein, Charles Conder and James Guthrie. During Kerr-Lawson's time, it was home to the sculptors Derwent Wood and Havard Thomas, the painters George Henry, Glyn Philpot and George Washington Lambert, the photographer Baron Adolphe de Meyer, the dancer Anton Dolin and

45. Edward Hutton, *Country Walks about Florence,* p. 11.

46. Ernest Samuels, *Bernard Berenson: The Making of a Connoisseur,* p. 310. The quotation is from Mary Berenson's diary, 3 November 1899.

47. Hewlett to Kerr-Lawson, 15 February 1897, Lawson family archives.

48. Maurice Hewlett, *Earthwork Out of Tuscany,* vol. 1, p. x.

49. George Sauter, "The International Society of Painters, Sculptors and Gravers," *The Studio,* August 1898, p. 110.

50. E. R. and J. Pennell, *The Life of James McNeill Whistler,* pp. 360-61; Pennell, *The Whistler Journal,* pp. 45-47.

Fig. 2   James and Caterina at Glebe Place

I shall take leave to say that no one knows his Italy better, or loves her more truly than he.[53]

Few of the works in the exhibition can now be firmly identified. Two views of Siena were reproduced with a review of the show and two of Venice, in an article he wrote on tempera, were probably part of it. The critics received his works respectfully. *The Times* described them as "extremely accomplished"[54] and *The Magazine of Art* as:

> examples of sincere craftsmanship applied to the expression of very well selected motives. He is [the critic continued] an artist with eminently correct taste, and his work has fine qualities of design and interpretation. Though . . . he dealt with material which has engaged the attention of many other painters, he treated it so discreetly, and with so much individuality that he succeeded in making it surprisingly attractive.[55]

The Athenaeum gave the most detailed discussion of the exhibition. After commenting on Kerr-Lawson being little known in England and having lived abroad, it praised the directness of his approach, especially his sensitive colouring, and noted his intimate sympathy with his motifs. A few works, such as the *Arno at Pisa* (no. 23), were "imposing, expressive of a strongly felt mood."[56]

Another group of works from about this time was a series of landscapes of Greece or Sicily. In a letter to Elizabeth Pennell in November 1904, Caterina states that her husband, "has just got a commission from a millionaire, a Mr. Loeb of New York, which may take us to Sicily or Greece in the spring as Loeb wants that sort of landscape."[57] The Mr. Loeb referred to is probably James Loeb, the retired banker and philanthropist, a Harvard classmate of Berenson's and founder of the Loeb Classical Library, published by Heinemann. Whether this commission was ever completed and what became of it is not known.

About 1903, Kerr-Lawson began a career as a mural painter. He had long been interested in the subject and had had long discussions about it with Watts. In November 1901, they had both been founding members of the Society of Painters in Tempera (now the Society of Mural Painters).[58]

Attempts to revive mural painting as a major decorative art, dated in Britain from the 1840s. Given the lack of a living tradition, however, existing styles and techniques were seldom adequate for artistic success. Given the great expense of murals, few could afford to commission them and those that were done were isolated efforts. Watts had done several and then had given up. The

the art nouveau architect Charles Rennie MacIntosh, who designed several of its houses.

With a stable income, a fixed home and a growing circle of friends, Kerr-Lawson finally bloomed and entered a highly productive period that would last through World War I. He now saw more of the Pennels, the De Morgans, the Hewletts and George Clausen. About 1904, he joined the Chelsea Arts Club and, in November 1907, the Art Workers Guild. He continued to be close to Watts and Whistler and once stayed at Limnerslease, Watts' Surrey home, doing etching and colour printing "compliments à la Signor."[51]

In April 1903, Kerr-Lawson held an exhibition of his *Little Landscapes of Italy,* at the Dowdeswell Galleries in London. These forty landscapes had been painted mainly in March and April 1902, while he and Maurice Hewlett had toured Italy.[52] Hewlett wrote a short introduction to the Dowdeswell catalogue. In it, he recalled their tour and remarked:

> Easy travel, light-hearted survey, attention for the genius of the place, love for the labourers in it; above all, respect and gratitude for the kindest, simplest and most honest folk in Europe, and their mellowed, weather-worn country—these were as much part of the artist's baggage as his tubes and canvases. Of the merits of Mr. Kerr-Lawson's work I have no title to speak, though they seem to me very considerable, but

51. Kerr-Lawson to Joseph Pennell, undated, Pennell Papers, Library of Congress, Washington, D.C.

52. Maurice Hewlett, *The Letters,* pp. 66-71.

53. *Little Landscapes of Italy,* Dowdeswell Galleries, London, April 1903.

54. "Minor Art Exhibitions," *The Times* (London), 14 April 1903.

55. "London Exhibitions," *The Magazine of Art,* June 1903, pp. 422-23.

56. "Messrs. Dowdeswell's Gallery," *The Athenaeum,* 11 April 1903, p. 473.

57. Caterina to Elizabeth Pennell, 26 November 1904, Pennell Papers.

58. Other founding members were Walter Crane, William Holman Hunt and Joseph Southall. Important early members were Edwin Austin Abbey, Robert Anning Bell and Sir William Blake Richmond.

importance of murals as part of a decorative scheme, however, was central to the philosophy of the Arts and Crafts Movement. During the late nineties, dreams of a revival seemed to be coming true. Prosperity and self-confidence triggered a vast building boom. Mural painters were improving their style and technique through the study of mediaeval and Renaissance precedents. Historicism would dominate the revival until its end in the 1920s. Painters in the classical tradition emphasized illusionistic space, chiaroscuro, and well modelled form while those in the mediaeval tradition the flatness of the wall surface, through large simple forms, strong outlines, rhythmic compositions and light, matt surfaces. Kerr-Lawson would be part of both traditions. His inspiration was classical yet, without being archaizing, he also aimed at flatness. In this he was similar to his friends Brangwyn and Clausen and to some of the followers of Puvis de Chavannes. Unlike Brangwyn, however, he had a restrained style, with little of the opulence and vigour that made Brangwyn so popular.

Kerr-Lawson's first and most important mural commission was for a series of decorations in Stoke Rochford Hall, the Lincolnshire home of Christopher Hatton Turnor. Turnor had been born and raised in Toronto and, graduating from Oxford in 1896, had studied architecture and settled in Surrey. He became a friend of his neighbour, George Watts, and in 1903-04 designed the Watts Gallery, on the painter's estate.[59] It was here he met Kerr-Lawson. Turnor had just inherited large family estates in Lincolnshire and was attempting to farm them in a modern, efficient way. In the process he would become a noted agricultural and social reformer with five major books to his credit.

Kerr-Lawson's murals were painted on canvas and let into wall panels in several Louis XV-style drawing rooms, where they formed a complete ensemble. They consisted of large Italian cityscapes, grisailles of peasants and animals and oval paper collages of genre and landscape subjects. A dozen of them were exhibited at the Alpine Club Gallery in June-July 1906, where they won him a reputation as "the English Canaletto."[60] The critic of *The Times* strongly emphasized that the panels should be regarded more as an ensemble than as individual works. "Looked at in that light," he wrote,

> those low-toned, smoothly painted, rather flat panels seen against white walls make up a beautiful scheme of decoration, interesting, restful and restrained. In all, the composition is broad and simple as it is to composition rather than atmosphere that the artist has devoted his attention. At the same time the colour is pure and the panels are so cunningly arranged with

Fig. 3

Illustrated above, but not included in the exhibition, are two of the over thirty mural panels created for Stoke Rochford Hall. The panels consisted of Italian, Spanish and Moroccan subjects, worked in oil, grisaille and paper collage. Fig. 3: Piazza San Firenze, a theme repeated in the "Italian

59. Mary Watts, *George Frederick Watts*, vol. 2, pp. 305-07.

60. The origin of the name is uncertain but it is repeated many times later.

Fig. 4

Set" (cat. no. 28). Fig. 4: The Forum, Rome, with the Temple of Saturn; a watercolour study is included in the exhibition (cat. no. 22). (For an example of an oval design see catalogue number 21; for a pair of grisailles, catalogue numbers 19 and 20.)

relation to each other that each gains something from its neighbours. The wall on the left of the visitor as he enters is particularly remarkable for the subtle gradations secured by arrangement.[61]

The Stoke Rochford panels remained in place until 1978, when they were sold by Turnor's niece at Christie's and scattered to the winds. Only a few of them are now located. They were important for providing a wealth of motifs for Kerr-Lawson's later works, for painted copies, lithographs and posters.

Seeing them now out of context, it is difficult to evaluate the panels as an ensemble. All share the same colours, scale and silhouetting of buildings against the sky. The repetition of these elements certainly would have added to a sense of unity and to the basic flatness of the wall surface. In subject, precision and composition, the comparison with the works of Canaletto is valid. Kerr-Lawson's panels are , nevertheless, far more broadly and simply painted. Compared to his earlier works, they are less realistic and more decorative and historical. The realism, however, is only modified rather than abandoned and they continue to show an interest in strong compositions and in effects of light and tone.

Shortly after his exhibition at the Alpine Club Gallery, Kerr-Lawson was commissioned by the Baron Aldenham to paint views of London for a small octagonal room in Aldenham House, near Elstree, Hertfordshire. Aldenham[62], a banker, scholar and art collector, painted twice by Watts, had seen the Stoke Rochford panels and wanted something similar. He and Kerr-Lawson settled on seven historic structures, mainly by Wren and Gibbs. These were: Horse Guards, London Bridge, St. Clement Danes, Hyde Park Corner, St. Paul's Cathedral, St. Margaret's, Westminster and St. Martin-in-the-Fields. These views of them were also painted on canvas and let into panels in the walls. The largest of them measured 84" x 56" and the smallest 36" x 35". Kerr-Lawson's approach to his subjects was similar to that in his Stoke Rochford panels. Most of these views were evenly and clearly lit, well composed and united by similar pearly, blue-grey tonalities. They too inspired lithographs and posters.

Lord Aldenham died in 1907, when the panels were being installed, and Kerr-Lawson was asked by his son, the Hon. Vicary Gibbs, to commemorate him with a marble bas-relief of his head after death. Kerr-Lawson was no sculptor[63] and the relief has since been lost. As remembered by the present Lord Aldenham, however, "It was gloomy beyond belief!"[64] As for the panels, they remained in position for many years but then were

61. "Exhibitions," *The Times*, 11 June 1906.

62. On Aldenham see *Dictionary of National Biography*, Second Supplement, vol. II, s.v.

63. Two other Kerr-Lawson sculptures are a bust of Caterina (Chelsea Library, London) and one of Lina Waterfield (British Institute of Florence).

64. Aldenham to Robert J. Lamb, 22 February 1979.

removed and now are owned by Aldenham's descendants in London.

In 1907-08 Kerr-Lawson became more active as a lithographer. He had long been interested in printmaking but what he produced is little known. Lithography had traditionally been the poor relation in the graphic arts. It was thought a commercial and reproductive process with little artistic potential of its own. Art dealers and collectors had little interest in it. During the eighties, Whistler had started making lithographs and, during the nineties, some younger artists had followed suit. In France, artistic lithography was having a strong revival. In Britain, it was younger, French-connected artists who seriously explored the medium. William Rothenstein, Charles Conder, Charles Shannon, and the Whistler circle all produced vital work at this time. *The Studio* gave its support but little commercial success ensued. Another such magazine was *The Neolith,* a short-lived but much admired quarterly of 1907-08, edited by F. Ernest Jackson and Gerald Spencer-Pryse. Many artists contributed illustrations to it. Kerr-Lawson contributed lithographs taken from his mural panels of St. Paul's Cathedral and *Il Colleone.*

When the contributors showed interest in forming a lithographers society, a meeting was held in Kerr-Lawson's Glebe Place studio.[65] The society was called the Senefelder Club, in honour of the inventor of lithography. Kerr-Lawson, Joseph Pennell, F. E. Jackson and A. S. Hartrick were its founders. They recruited new members, rented a studio and bought a second-hand press on which to print their works. Pennell became President and threw his prodigious energies into organizing exhibitions and writing books and articles. The first exhibition was in 1910 and many followed thereafter. Pennell gave the Club an international name, with exhibitions not just in Britain but in Germany, Italy, Belgium, the United States, Canada, India, Australia and New Zealand.

Kerr-Lawson's major works done through the Club were the "Italian Set," the "Spanish Set," a set made from the Aldenham panels and some head and shoulders portraits of friends. The "Italian Set" (cat. nos. 24-33) was a series of ten lithotints (fifty impressions each) done in 1908 and based on panels in Stoke Rochford Hall. The "Spanish Set" (also known as "The Spanish Gypsy"), was made up of six lithographs, based on a variety of Spanish genre paintings. Three of his portraits were of Joseph Pennell (cat. no. 39), William De Morgan (cat. no. 40) and Maurice Hewlett (cat. no. 42). All of his lithographs received a good press. The print expert, Malcolm Salaman, for instance, writing in 1919, said:

> When Mr. Kerr-Lawson draws a place you know all about it, for his eye is pictorially observant of the living detail as well as the general aspect, and he has all the nuances of lithography at command.[66]

Another expert, Sir Frederick Wedmore, stated:

> A propos the publication by Mr. Kerr-Lawson of a series of lithotints—The Italian Set—I am reminded that I included his name as that of one amongst only three or four men in regard to whom there was good reason to suppose—it may be even good reason to know—that they are capable of doing large decorative work, important, dignified, significant, and thoroughly individual . . . Mr. Whistler is probably the only artist of our time who has used the lithographic stone for wash drawings as significant and successful as those of Mr. Kerr-Lawson.[67]

Stemming from Kerr-Lawson's Senefelder Club connections came a chance to design posters for London Transport. Frank Pick, the Chairman of the company, was famous for promoting high quality design.[68] Other Club members who also designed for him were Hartrick, Jackson, Pryse and Brangwyn. Kerr-Lawson's two designs, from 1913 and 1915, were for sepia toned posters. The first was of St. Martin-in-the-Fields (cat. no. 58) and the second of Westminster Abbey and St. Margaret's Church. They were part of a campaign to get the public to rediscover London, through sightseeing on the Underground. When the campaign posters appeared, they created quite a stir.[69] Kerr-Lawson would design posters once again, during the late 1920s, for the Empire Marketing Board. Some of these are included in this exhibition (cat. nos. 70, 71, 72).

Besides being active as a painter and lithographer, Kerr-Lawson spent much of his time as a dealer and expert in the old masters. These works came to have a strong influence on his own oeuvre. His specialty was the Italian primitives of the trecento and quattrocento, though he dealt in a wider range of works. He was small fry in the field but still he moved in such expert company as Herbert Horne, Roger Fry and Charles Ricketts. He seldom dealt in great works but occasionally made a "find." Like those of many dealers, his attributions were sometimes questioned.[70] Most of the works he dealt in can neither be identified nor located. The major exception is El Greco's, *The Adoration of the Shepherds,* now in the Metropolitan Museum of Art in New York. An early copy of Hieronymous Bosch's *Christ Crowned with Thorns* is now in the collection of his nephew, Dr. J. A. L. McCullough, and a workshop version of Taddeo Gaddi's *Madonna and Child Enthroned* is now in the Yale University Art Gallery. Works attributed to Bonifazio de Pitati, Rembrandt

---

65. The two prime sources for information on the Club are A. S. Hartrick, *A Painter's Pilgrimage Through Fifty Years,* Joseph Pennell, "The Senefelder Club and the Revival of Artistic Lithography," *The Studio,* February 1914, pp. 3-6.

66. Malcolm C. Salaman, *Modern Woodcuts and Lithographs,* pp. 123-24.

67. Quoted from *Pall Mall Gazette* by Hector Charlesworth, "Praise for Canadian Painter," *Saturday Night,* 3 October 1914, p. 3.

68. On Pick and his patronage see Christian Barman, *The Man Who Built London Transport* and Michael Levey, *London Transport Posters.*

69. Walter Shaw Sparrow, *Advertising and British Art,* p. 134.

70. An example of this is seen in Roger Fry, *The Letters,* vol. 1, pp. 218-19.

69   *Cheyne Walk, Carlyle's Statue, Cheyne Row and Archdeacon Bevan*   [undated]

(a collection of etchings), Tintoretto, Boltraffio, Moroni and Zoffany are all supposed to have passed through Kerr-Lawson's hands. He also served as artistic advisor to his brother Andrew, whose collection was given to the University Art Museum in Berkeley, California. In it were works attributed to Ribera, Rembrandt, Hals, Steen, Ostade, Kneller, Lely, Hogarth, Gainsborough, Romney, Constable and Turner.[71]

Stemming from Kerr-Lawson's expertise were several magazine articles on artistic subjects. The first, on tempera painting, appeared in *The Magazine of Art* in September 1903. Kerr-Lawson was a charming writer, in the belleletristic style of his day and, though his article was technical, it is easily read.

The second article under his name appeared in the new *Burlington Magazine*. Its content was slight but well formed—a footnote to nineteenth century Anglo-Italian art history. Its subject was two portraits—one by Watts, the other by Alfred Stevens—of the picturesque Anglo-Florentine character, the Cavaliere William Blundell Spence.

In a third article, in the same magazine, Kerr-Lawson tackled a weightier subject. Here he tried to prove that a Lorenzo Lotto portrait, in the Kunsthistorische Museum in Vienna, was actually a self-portrait.

His most substantial written work was a long essay on "The Influence of the Franciscan Legend on Italian Art." This appeared in 1908, in *Assisi of St. Francis,* a book by his friend Clarissa Goff. As usual, it is well-written, is based on extensive knowledge of the works concerned and is illuminating on fine points of style and technique. Nearly seventy-five years later, it is still well worth reading, even for professionals.

In 1912, Kerr-Lawson exhibited works with the Canadian Art Club, in Toronto, and thus reestablished contact with Canada. On leaving Canada in 1887, he had ceased to exhibit actively and soon had been dropped from membership in the Royal Canadian Academy. His works had appeared occasionally in mixed exhibitions and he had kept in touch with his family and friends like Homer Watson. He was known more by reputation than by works, a reputation as one of Canada's notable expatriates, who had to go abroad to realize his ideals. In 1907, when Edmund Morris and Curtis Williamson had founded the Canadian Art Club, one of their aims had been to enliven the artistic scene by luring expatriate talent home. In his opening speech, at the first Club exhibition, the Honorary President, D. R. Wilkie, had asked:

How often have we heard the statement there is no art in Canada! To prove this statement false, we have only to turn to the official lists of the Salon of France, to the Royal Academy, to the International Society of London, to the Royal Institute of Glasgow, to the National Academy of New York and to various international exhibitions thruout[sic] the world to find that Canadians have held and do hold positions of respect and honour amongst the world's great painters. Such men as Paul Peel, [Sir James Jebusa] Shannon, Blair Bruce, J. Kerr-Lawson, [Frederick C. V.] Ede, Mrs. Stanhope Forbes and Mary Bell Eastlake and the sculptors [Louis-Philippe] Hébert, [Alfred] Laliberté and [A. Phimister] Proctor are only a few of those who have brought honour to their native land and renown to themselves.[72]

Another example of the high esteem Kerr-Lawson had won in Canada is the following summary of his career which appeared in *Saturday Night.* "Many will be interested to learn," it states:

of the eminent position that has been won abroad for the Canadian painter J. Kerr-Lawson, a former resident of Toronto, who has for some years lived in England . . . Mr. Kerr-Lawson devotes himself to architectural painting and to the highest order of lithography in which he is a worthy follower of Whistler. Many of his works of the latter class have won high encomiums from British and Continental critics. As an oil painter, his beautiful colouring and thin smooth brushwork are unique . . . In all quarters this Torontonian is recognized as an artist who has, in the fullest sense of the word, "arrived".[73]

Kerr-Lawson was invited to exhibit with the Club through its President, Homer Watson, and, in 1912, he

Fig. 5 Arras *(mural in the Senate Chamber, Ottawa)*

71. Francis E. Vaughan, *Andrew C. Lawson,* pp. 221-25.

72. "Canadian Art is Given Fresh Stimulus," *Toronto World,* 4 February 1908.

73. Hector Charlesworth, "The Pictures of James Kerr-Lawson," *Saturday Night,* 20 June 1914, p. 4.

and W. H. Clapp were elected "Painter Members." Of his five Sicilian subjects in the 1912 exhibition, the critic of *The News* commented they were "very fine examples of his mature technical powers" and that:

> Mr. J. K. Lawson seems to have abandoned the practice of heavy underpainting for decisively imposed pure thin colour. It has been suggested that this change of manner has been due to his having recently been engaged upon some large decorative works. This may be, but the studies he has sent do not lack in pictorial quality. They are well composed and the colour, though flat, is luminous and airy.[74]

In 1913, Kerr-Lawson exhibited two larger paintings with the Club: *Boston* (cat. no. 51) and *Winter in Kent* (now unlocated). The critic of *The Globe* described these as "patiently and carefully done, though a trifle photographic."[75] The young Lawren Harris, writing in *The Year Book of Canadian Art,* was much more positive. After discussing the work of Ernest Lawson, of New York, he commented:

> Then there is the other Lawson (J. Kerr), now of London, England. His "Boston" (in Lincolnshire), in which an old square towered church looks over the fen country, is unusual in draughtsmanship and felicity of colour. He is exact, almost to the point of being meticulous. But the stuff is there, and his thin pigments are as delicate as a water-colour.[76]

In 1915, fifteen of Kerr-Lawson's lithographs from the Italian and Spanish Sets and from the English series were included in the last Club exhibition. They were little noticed, though Hector Charlesworth, writing as the Canadian contributor to *The Studio*, described them as "his exquisite lithographs, the fame of which had already

Fig. 6 The Cloth Hall, Ypres
(mural in the Senate Chamber, Ottawa)

crossed the Atlantic."[77] Charlesworth, a lay-member of the Club and critic and editor of *Saturday Night,* kept Kerr-Lawson well before the Canadian public after 1914. With the heightened imperialism created by the war, his reputation reached its Canadian apogee.

The outbreak of the war saw the lives of the Kerr-Lawsons little changed. They could not travel abroad but were otherwise unrestricted. As it dragged on, they became more involved. Caterina was a volunteer in Queen Mary's Hostel for Nurses. In 1916, Kerr-Lawson and other distinguished artists designed commemorative stamps to be sold for the benefit of the British Red Cross Fund. His one known design (cat. no. 61), a lithograph titled *What I Gave I Have,* has a simple image of a British nursing sister bandaging the arm of a wounded soldier. He also designed a lithographed recruiting poster (cat. no. 60).

In 1916-17, Kerr-Lawson undertook his largest wartime commission. He was made a Major with Lord Beaverbrook's Canadian War Records Office and directed to paint works documenting the war effort. During the summer and fall, he was in Belgium, quartered at "The Nine Elms," a house at Poperinghe, near Ypres and at the Saskatoon Club in Arras.[78] Here he made studies for his two large paintings, *Arras, the Dead City* and *The Cloth Hall, Ypres.* These were worked up in his Glebe Place studio and, by March 1918, he could report that one of them was "now well on on the way to completion."[79] A photo of him in uniform, working on *Arras...,* was taken about this time and reproduced in *Saturday Night.* He was also approached to work for the British and for the Australians. While nothing came of the former, he did complete for the latter a painting titled *Refugees Returning to Cambrai under Protection of an Australian Trooper.* It is now in the Art Gallery of New South Wales in Sydney. He also painted a portrait of an Australian soldier, Major J. S. S. Anderson, D.S.O., M.C. Titled *The Warrior,* it was exhibited widely and given to the National Gallery of Canada after his death.

After the war ended, Kerr-Lawson's two large Canadian paintings [figs. 5 and 6] were designated part of a larger mural scheme for the Senate Chamber in the newly rebuilt Parliament building in Ottawa. Before they were installed, however, they and other war paintings were exhibited, in 1919 and 1920, at the Royal Academy in London, in New York, Ottawa and Toronto. The catalogue accompanying them took a lofty and severe tone, castigating the Germans for their sins. In discussing *Arras . . .,* for instance, it stated that:

74. "Canadian Art Club's 5th Exhibition," *The News,* undated.

75. "Fine Pictures at the Canadian Art Club Show," *The Globe,* 10 May 1913.

76. Lawren Harris, "The Canadian Art Club," in *The Year Book of Canadian Art 1913,* p. 214.

77. Hector Charlesworth, "Studio Talk: Toronto," *The Studio,* May 1916, p. 274.

78. Caterina on note attached to 1920 Information Form, Kerr-Lawson clippings file, National Gallery of Canada Library.

79. Kerr-Lawson to Alfred Yockney, 23 March 1918, Imperial War Museum, London.

The painting brings home . . . a sense of the appalling devastation wrought over hundreds of miles of French and Belgian territory by the Germans, and the terrible danger to which France and Civilization are constantly exposed. The Church, whose ruins are in the foreground, is the Cathedral Church of Arras. It is named St. Vaast, after the saint who devoted his life to rebuilding the sacred places destroyed by the Barbarians over eight hundred years ago.[80]

An unofficial, artistic view of the paintings came from Hector Charlesworth, in his review of the exhibition. "Mr. Lawson," he wrote:

is one of the painters with whom Gerald Moira and George Clausen should also be included, who have definitely succeeded in painting pieces that will certainly harmonize with a noble architectural design. Mr. Lawson's colour sense, his perfection in drawing and marvelously transparent brushwork, have never been more happily exemplified. 'Arras' is in lower tones than its companion piece 'Ypres' . . . but decorative in the noblest sense. Its pearly grey colour scheme seems to augment the sense of desolation and a human touch is given to the whole by the black clad woman, standing lonely amidst the ruins, her figure reflected in a shell hole filled with water.[81]

Younger artists, though, like Arthur Lismer, were critical of the academicism and "foolish panoply of war"[82] they saw in many of the War Memorial paintings, Kerr-Lawson's among them. While praising the works of A. Y. Jackson and Fred Varley, Harold Gilman and D. Y. Cameron, Lismer described *The Cloth Hall, Ypres* as "a papery photographic rendering, absolutely without a single passage of dramatic value, possessing neither volume nor weight."[83] By the Group of Seven's standards, *Ypres* and *Arras* are certainly precise, papery, weightless and academic. In comparison to many other War Memorial paintings they are aloof, neither revelling in the "foolish panoply of war" nor revealing the dead and maimed in the trenches. Their bold compositions and contrasting colours, however, do make them dramatic and, as mural decorations within the Senate, they are far more successful than the over-sized easel paintings that surround them. If only Kerr-Lawson had been asked to decorate the whole Chamber!

While the growth of artistic nationalism during the twenties led to a decline in Kerr-Lawson's Canadian reputation, in Britian he was enjoying some official recognition. In 1922, he and Brangwyn organized the British section of the Venice Biennale. Though their selection included Mark Gertler and C. R. W. Nevinson, it was, on the whole, conservative, with George Clausen, Augustus John, William Nicholson and Walter Sickert being their typical choices. Kerr-Lawson also enjoyed

social success. He and Caterina were fervent lovers of music and the theatre and were often lent a box at the Drury Lane Theatre by the then Duke of Bedford. James was a friend of the diva, Eva Turner, knew Pablo Casals, and painted a portrait of the then well known Anglo-Spanish cellist, Agustin Rubio (Ferens Art Gallery, Hull). He and Caterina mingled with the more intellectual members of the aristocracy, such as the diplomat Lord Lothian and Lord and Lady Desborough.[84]

By far their most notable friendship was with Queen Mary. Caterina had met her through her work with the nurses' hostel during the war and used every ounce of her charm to gain the Queen's patronage. Royal visits to Kerr-Lawson's studio and exhibitions followed as did purchases and gifts of work, the exchange of Christmas presents and a correspondence lasting over thirty years.[85] Among the purchases and gifts were the painting of Florence (cat. no. 45) included in this exhibition, the "Italian Set" of lithotints, and a large lithograph of St. Martin-in-the-Fields. The most interesting of the lot was a tiny lithograph of a man with a walking stick standing in front of a house. (Royal Archives, Windsor Castle.) This was done in 1924 for the decoration of the Queen's famous doll house.[86] Sir Edwin Lutyens designed the house and many well-known artists and writers equipped it with miniature versions of their works.

In 1924, Kerr-Lawson was also commissioned to make two large paper mosaics for the chapel in the Palace of Arts of the British Empire Exhibition at Wembley. One showed *The Annunciation* (cat. no. 65) and the other *The Adoration of the Shepherds.* He had already used the paper mosaic technique in oval panels at Stoke Rochford House but here it was used on a mural scale, for a flat, decorative effect. Paper mosaic is essentially collage but, while flatness is part of each, nothing could be further from cubist collage than Kerr-Lawson's two panels. With their large central arches dominating their compositions, they show his debt to Fra Angelico and other quattrocento painters.

In 1926 and 1930, he had two successful exhibitions in the Beaux Arts Gallery. Both consisted mainly of views of Italy, Spain and Morocco and both were well received. Most reviewers commented on fine drawing, flat tonalities and decorative effects and quiet, delicate subtleties. Typical were the critics of *The Times* and *The Illustrated London News,* who wrote that Kerr-Lawson's works bore the "stamp of an interesting personality, both alert and fastidious, more concerned to say the thing rightly than to force it upon the attention,"[87] or that they showed a "very

80. Percy Francis Godenrath, *Lest We Forget,* p. 31.

81. Hector Charlesworth, "Reflections," *Saturday Night,* 18 September 1920, p. 2.

82. Arthur Lismer, "The Canadian War Memorials," *The Rebel,* October 1919, p. 40.

83. Ibid., p. 41.

84. Much of the Desborough correspondence is in the Lawson family archives.

85. Much of the Queen Mary correspondence is in the Lawson family archives.

86. Elizabeth Lambert, "Queen Mary's Doll's House," *Architectural Digest,* December 1981, pp. 84-89.

87. "Art Exhibitions: Mr. Kerr-Lawson," *The Times,* 26 January 1926, p. 17.

distinct individuality, which stamps them as the product of an original mind but . . . no trace of the anxious experiments and risky adventures that have revolutionized the art of today."[88]

During the twenties and thirties, Kerr-Lawson worked increasingly as a portraitist. His Renaissance influenced historicism was here very obvious. Typical are his portraits of Andrew Lawson (cat. no. 68), Mrs. Cawthra (cat. no. 79), and Frank Brangwyn (cat. no. 81).

His portrait of Brangwyn is probably the best of all of these portraits. Brangwyn's face and body are true likenesses though his pose and setting are decorative and symbolic. As do sitters in Botticelli portraits, he holds up a medallion showing Kerr-Lawson's head. The inscription on the medallion and in the lower right corner of the portrait testify to the depth of their friendship. The plain area of colour, placed arbitrarily behind Brangwyn's head to give it more prominence, is likewise taken from Renaissance sources. The decorative quality of the portrait, however, its firm composition and carefully limited colour scheme, is derived from the *Japoniste* tradition then very popular. Brangwyn especially loved Japanese art and the screen in the background was typical of his tastes. Its exotic cranes may also refer to the many similar birds Brangwyn himself painted, in his famous British Empire Panels.

Kerr-Lawson's last large project was a never completed series of five mural panels for the hall of White Lodge, the Hampstead home of Col. A. C. R. Waite and the Hon. Mrs. Waite. Mrs. Waite, heiress to the Austin automobile fortune, had befriended Caterina and became her husband's main collector and patroness. The subjects of the panels were mainly Moroccan ones and the compositions pastiches of earlier works. In *Fortune* (cat. no. 82) and *The Mirage* (Alghanim Collection, Windsor, England), the effect was charming. Kerr-Lawson was still at work on the remaining panels when he died.

Death came on Monday, May 1, 1939, after a cerebral hemorrhage. Many newspapers in Scotland, England and Canada carried his obituary. All stressed the point that, with his retiring nature and his expatriation, Kerr-Lawson was less well known than he deserved. Of the tributes to his character that appeared, a typical one was that published in *The Times,* which said:

> Kerr-Lawson's character was as delicately fastidious as his art. He had the true modesty which would neither advertise himself nor encourage others to advertise him, and praise made him uneasy. His knowledge of painting was profound, his judgement penetrating and illuminating, but he always

had to be asked for it. He had the liveliest interest in everyday affairs and applied to them a whimsical sophistry which always threw an unexpected light on them, but often failed to hide his unchanging sympathy with the poor and the oppressed. Generous and kind and gentle, he was the least self-seeking of friends, and that was why he made so many in every rank of life wherever he was and wherever he went.[89]

His funeral was held at Chelsea Old Church on May 4. Eva Turner sang his favourite selections from *Aida* and over eighty of his friends attended. His body was cremated at Golders Green cemetery.

Caterina lived on thirteen years after him. Without him to restrain her, she worked determinedly to secure his place in history. The best of his remaining works she gave to various art museums in Britain and Canada. Some she gathered together for seven memorial exhibitions in public and commercial galleries. In 1940, she was awarded a civil list pension of £100., in recognition of her financial state as well as her husband's services to art. She started going blind but her spirits seldom flagged and her correspondence with such younger friends as David Carritt, Adrian Bury and Lina Waterfield was lively. The end finally came of heart failure, on June 11, 1952. Her funeral was private and she was cremated at Golders Green on June 13.

With Caterina's death, Kerr-Lawson's reputation practically disappeared. It was a difficult time for Victorian artists and most of his contemporaries suffered equally through the change in critical values. Today the Victorians are far more respected and there is a swell of interest in older Canadian artists. The time is ripe for Kerr-Lawson's reputation to be, in part, restored.

Kerr-Lawson is interesting on many levels. He led an exciting, multifaceted life and moved in important artistic and literary circles. He maintained the British tradition in Canadian culture well into this century. He worked on a broad range of subjects in an equally broad range of media and, most importantly, created many fine works. These are distinguished by a bold sense of decorative composition combined with a subtlety in the treatment of light, tone, colour and space. These works certainly merit inclusion in our Canadian artistic heritage.

Robert J. Lamb
Winnipeg
September, 1982

88. "Italy Seen by Scottish Artist of European Repute," *The Illustrated London News,* 13 February 1926, p. 261.

89. "Letter of Tribute," *The Times,* 4 May 1939, p. 21.

Fig. 7   The artist (standing) with Frank Brangwyn   ca. 1927

CATALOGUE

(All sizes are image size unless otherwise stated, and are given in centimetres and inches with height preceding width.)

1. **Portrait of Alice Margaret Lawson**   ca. 1882-83

   oil on canvas   40 x 30.7   (15¾ x 12)

   Collection of Miss Norah McCullough, Guelph, Ontario

   Notes: Alice Margaret Lawson (1867-1949) was one of Kerr-Lawson's younger sisters. She later became a nurse and married Dr. John W. S. McCullough of Toronto. A note on the back of the portrait claims that Alice was fifteen and Kerr-Lawson twenty-one when it was painted. If true, this indicates it was painted on Kerr-Lawson's visit home from Paris, mentioned in Blair Bruce's letter of 11 December 1883.

1

2. **Fannie**   1885

   oil on canvas   50.7 x 40.5   (19⅞ x 15⅞)

   Collection of the National Gallery of Canada, Ottawa

   Notes: The sitter is probably Caterina's half sister, Frances (Fannie) Bell Smith, born in Hamilton on 26 April 1874 and, thus, eleven years old when the portrait was painted. By the 1920s, Fannie was resident in Torquay, Devonshire and continued there through the 1940s. The portrait was likely a gift to William Brymner, as it came from his descendants to the National Gallery. It was probably exhibited at the Ontario Society of Artists in 1885 (no. 18).

2

3. **"Music, when soft voices die, Vibrates in the memory."** — *Shelley*   ca. 1885

   oil on canvas   56.3 x 69   (22⅛ x 27⅛)

   Collection of the Art Gallery of Windsor, Windsor, Ontario

   Gift of Mr. and Mrs. William N. Tepperman, 1978

   References: "Royal Academy Exhibition," *The Citizen* (Ottawa), 3 February 1886; *An exhibition of selected major acquisitions 1978-1980,* Art Gallery of Windsor, Windsor, 1980, repr.

   Notes: The sitters were daughters of James Cummings, once Mayor of Hamilton, Ontario, and were shown in their family home. Alice Cummings plays the piano while Louise, later a distinguished mathematics professor, sings. The painting was exhibited at the Ontario Society of Artists in 1885 (no. 35) and at the Royal Canadian Academy in 1886 (no. 130).

3

4. **Portrait of James Smith**   ca. 1886

   oil on canvas   56.5 x 45.7   (22¼ x 18)

   Collection of the Art Gallery of Ontario, Toronto

   Gift of the Ontario Society of Artists, 1947

   Notes: Smith (1832-1918), was a Scottish born architect and painter who came to Canada as a youth. He was a pupil of William Thomas in Toronto and designed old Knox College in that city. He painted landscapes and marines and was Treasurer of the Royal Canadian Academy from 1880 to 1887 and 1910 to 1914. This portrait was exhibited at the Royal Canadian Academy in 1886 (no. 185).

4

5. **Horse and Cart on Rural Road**   November 1886
oil on canvas   27.5 x 38.1   (10⅞ x 15)
Collection of the University of Guelph, Macdonald Stewart
Art Centre, Guelph, Ontario
Gift of Alumni, Alma Mater Fund 1975

References: Sotheby and Co. (Canada) Ltd., *Important Canadian Paintings...,* 20-21 October 1975, lot 191; Judith M. Nasby, *The University of Guelph Art Collection,* no. 75.48, p. 193, repr.

Notes: This is a typical early plein-air landscape, especially well composed. It may be the same as *A Country Road,* at The Industrial Exhibition, Toronto, 1898, no. 285, or *A Roadway,* loaned by C. W. Irwin to the Canadian National Exhibition, Toronto, 1907, no. 79.

5

6. **La Caterina**   ca. 1887
oil on canvas   197 x 98.8   (77⅝ x 38⅞)
Collection of the National Gallery of Canada, Ottawa

References: "Picture from the past," *Evening Standard* (London), 17 March 1947; Francis E. Vaughan, *Andrew C. Lawson,* pp. 33, 35, repr.; Sotheby's Belgravia, *Victorian Paintings, Drawings and Watercolours,* 25 July 1978, lot 228, repr.; Sotheby's Belgravia, *Victorian Paintings, Drawings and Watercolours,* 28 November 1978, lot 173, repr.

Notes: This portrait of Caterina was probably painted in Hamilton and, with its sure design and subtle tonal relationships, is one of the strongest works Kerr-Lawson ever did. It was lost for many years and rediscovered in an attic about 1947. It was later owned by the Waites and was probably included in the Institut Français d'Ecosse exhibition of 1952 (no. 2). Other portraits of Caterina include a painting in the University Art Museum, Berkeley, a lithograph with Dr. Douglas Kerr-Lawson, Waterloo and a bust in the Chelsea Library, London.

6

7. **The Artist's Mother in Wicker Chair**   [undated]
oil on canvas   60.96 x 84.12   (24 x 33⅛)
Collection of the University Art Museum, University of
California, Berkeley, California
Andrew C. Lawson Bequest

References: Francis E. Vaughan, *Andrew C. Lawson,* p. 223.

Notes: This scene of his mother and her friends in a sewing circle was probably painted during the mid- to late 1880s. Its composition and colour tonalities relate to those of *Music...* and Jessie's age and appearance seem consistent with this date.

7

8. **Learning to Read**   [undated]
oil on canvas   48.3 x 34.3   (19 x 13½)
Collection of Dr. J. A. L. McCullough, McMurray, Pennsylvania

Notes: This small genre scene probably dates from the 1880s or early 1890s.

8

9. **Mediterranean Coast, Morocco**   1888

oil on wood panel   12.5 x 22   (4⅞ x 8⅝)

Collection of the National Gallery of Canada, Ottawa

Notes: This painting was probably exhibited at the Royal Canadian Academy in 1889 (no. 13).

9

10. **Study of a Girl**   1888

oil on canvas   34.6 x 27   (13⅝ x 10⅝)

Collection of Beaverbrook Art Gallery, Fredericton, N.B.

Gift of Mr. and Mrs. G. Blair Laing

References: Beaverbrook Art Gallery: Paintings, Fredericton, 1959, p. 20.

Notes: The identity of the girl is unknown. So is that of the Judge Clark in the inscription "To my Friend Judge Clark," in the upper right corner. Presumably they are relatives. Though Kerr-Lawson was in Scotland in 1888, the form of address "Judge" implies a Canadian judge. The painting also emerged from Canadian sources later on. The Judge may be Judge George Mackenzie Clark, Q.C. (1828-?) of Cobourg and Toronto, who, in 1888, was appointed chief solicitor to the Canadian Pacific Railway. This painting was shown in an *Exhibition of Paintings by Old and Modern Masters* at the University of New Brunswick in 1955 (no. 20), and in *The Figure in Canadian Painting,* organized by the Beaverbrook Art Gallery in 1972 (no. 5).

10

11. **St. Monance Harbour**   1890

oil   16.5 x 24.1   (6½ x 9½)

Collection of Mrs. Peter F. Groff, Andover, Massachusetts

Notes: St. Monance, where Jessie Lawson was raised, was a fishing port only several miles from Pittenweem and Anstruther.

11

12. **Farm Work in Scotland**   1890

oil on canvas   35.7 x 52.8   (14 x 20¾)

Collection of Dr. Dorothy J. McCullough, Toronto, Ontario

Notes: This work may well be related to *Potato Harvest in Fife,* exhibited at the Glasgow Institute in 1890.

12

13. **Poor Sue—on a Farm in Kirkudbrightshire**   1890

pastel on paper   30.5 x 24.2   (12 x 9½)

Collection of The Fine Art Society Limited, London, England

References: Sotheby's Belgravia, *Victorian Paintings, Drawings and Watercolours,* 9 January 1979, lot 145 repr.; Peyton Skipwith, *The Rustic Image,* no. 30, repr.; "Current and Forthcoming Exhibitions," *The Burlington Magazine,* November, 1979, p. 739, repr., no. 82.

Notes: A note on the back of this work says it was drawn on a farm in Kirkudbrightshire. It is probably the same work as no. 76 in the 1948 Heffer Gallery exhibition, no. 8 in the 1949 Annan exhibition and no. 49 in the 1952 Institut Français d'Ecosse exhibition. It was lent to the last of these exhibitions by a Mr. and Mrs. Charles Williams.

13

14. **Portrait of Paul Verlaine**   ca. 1894

oil on canvas   42.6 x 32.4   (16¾ x 12¾)

Collection of the Fitzwilliam Museum, Cambridge University, Cambridge, England

References: Hector Charlesworth, "The Kerr-Lawson Show in London," *Saturday Night,* 27 March 1926, p. 3; Frederick Whyte, *William Heinemann: A Memoir,* pp. 41-42; "James Kerr-Lawson: Funeral of Famous Artist," *West London Press,* 12 May 1939; James Kerr-Lawson, "A Newly Discovered Portrait of Verlaine," *Apollo,* May — June 1939, pp. 262-63, repr.; Francis Carco, *Verlaine,* p. 100, pl XI; "London News and Comment: Kerr-Lawson Pictures," *The Scotsman* (Edinburgh), 5 November 1942; "Art Exhibitions," *The Times* (London), 11 November 1942, p. 6; "Verlaine Portrait — Publisher's Inspiration," *Daily Telegraph* (London), 11 February 1943; "Verlaine Portrait to Fitzwilliam Museum," *The Times* (London), 13 February 1943, p. 8, repr.; Francis E. Vaughan, *Andrew C. Lawson,* p. 33; J. W. Goodison, *Fitzwilliam Museum Cambridge, Catalogue of Paintings, Vol. III, The British School,* no. 2507, p. 143.

Notes: This portrait was included in the Beaux Arts Gallery exhibition of 1942 and in the Institut Français d'Ecosse exhibition of 1952 (no. 10) and was sold by Caterina to the Fitzwilliam Museum in 1943. The charcoal drawing on which it is based is in the collection of Mme. G. R. Varin, Versailles, France. The drawing was reproduced in *Colour,* February 1922, p. 13 and in *The Connoisseur,* June 1952, p. 115.

Exhibited in Guelph, Windsor, Toronto, Calgary and Fredericton.

14

15. **The Smithy, Glasgow**   [undated]

watercolour on paper   35.56 x 50.16   (14 x 19⅝)

Collection of the University Art Museum, University of California, Berkeley, California

Andrew C. Lawson Bequest

References: Francis E. Vaughan, *Andrew C. Lawson,* p. 224.

Notes: One of the only works associated with Kerr-Lawson's Glasgow period, this painting probably dates from about 1891 to 1898.

15

16. **Portrait of Henry James Ross**   ca. 1901-02

tempera on canvas   101 x 78   (39¾ x 30¾)

Private collection

References: J. Kerr-Lawson, "Tempera: A New Light on an Old Method," *The Magazine of Art,* September 1903, p. 562, repr.; Janet Ross, *The Fourth Generation,* pp. 338-39, repr.

Notes: Henry James Ross (1820-1902) was an Anglo-Egyptian banker, author of *Letters from the East* (1902) and husband of the writer Janet Ross (1842-1927). He and his wife and their niece, Lina Waterfield, were close Florentine friends of the Kerr-Lawsons. This portrait was included in the International Art Exhibition, Dusseldorf, 1904 (no. 2065). Kerr-Lawson also made a silverpoint portrait and a bust of Lina Waterfield. The former is unlocated and the latter is in the British Institute of Florence.

16

17. **Maurice Henry Hewlett**   1904

oil on canvas   37.5 x 51.4   (14¾ x 20¼)

Collection of the National Portrait Gallery, London, England

References: K. K. Yung, *National Portrait Gallery: Complete Illustrated Catalogue 1856-1979,* no. 2800, p. 275, repr.

Notes: Maurice Henry Hewlett (1861-1923) was a novelist, poet and essayist, famous during the Edwardian period for his historical romances, *The Forest Lovers* (1898), *The Life of Richard Yea-and-Nay* (1900) and *The Queen's Quair* (1904) and for his epic poem *The Song of the Plow* (1916). The portrait was painted at the Casa di Boccaccio during the spring of 1904, when Hewlett was visiting. A pencil study for it is also in the National Portrait Gallery and a lithograph after it is in the Art Gallery of Ontario.

17

18. Il Ponte, Scuola di San Marco, Venice

ca. 1903-08
oil on canvas   139.7 x 116.8   (55 x 46)
Collection of Mrs. John McConville, London, England

References: Caterina to Elizabeth Pennell, 26 November 1904, Pennell Papers; "Exhibitions," *The Times* (London), 11 June 1906; Hector Charlesworth, "The Pictures of J. Kerr-Lawson," *Saturday Night,* 20 June 1914, p. 4, repr.; Grace D. Ruthenburg, "J.B. Speed Museum Notes," *Louisville Courier-Journal,* 18 October 1931; "Speed Museum Panel Display Attracts Many," *Louisville Herald-Post,* 19 October 1931; Queen Mary to Caterina, 1 May 1934, Lawson Family Archives; Christopher Turnor, "Letters," *The Times* (London), 6 May 1939; Nikolaus Pevsner and John Harris, *The Buildings of England: Lincolnshire,* pp. 643-45; Francis E. Vaughan, *Andrew C. Lawson,* p. 33; Christie Manson and Woods Ltd., *Fine Victorian Pictures,* 21 July 1978, lots 64-74, repr.; Christie Manson and Woods Ltd., *Fine Victorian Pictures,* 13 October 1978, lots 92-103, repr.; Christie's South Kensington, *Sale of English and Continental Pictures,* 14 May 1980, lot 322.

Notes: This is one of the more than thirty mural panels executed for Christopher Hatton Turnor at Stoke Rochford Hall. The work began in 1903 and extended over about a thirty year period. How the panels were arranged on the walls is not known. Among the others, and not repeated in the "Italian Set," were *The Baptistry in Pistoia, The Pyramid of Cestius and Porto San Paolo, Rome, The Arch of Titus, Rome* and a variety of Spanish peasant and Moroccan genre subjects, done in grisaille and paper collage. When the panels were sold at Christie's in 1978, they were scattered, and only a handful are now located. They inspired "The Italian Set" of lithographs and also four large painted copies, done about 1930 and formerly in the Speed Art Museum, Louisville, Kentucky.
 The Capriccio . . . (cat. no. 21) was originally installed under the mural panel of *San Giorgio Maggiore, Venice.* The two grisaille studies (cat. nos. 19, 20), along with two others, now with Waldheim Old Master Paintings, Hambledon, Hampshire, England, later provided motifs for sections of the Empire Marketing Board poster, during the late twenties.

18

19. Women, Children and a Man Milking a Goat

[undated]
grisaille on canvas   49.5 x 118.1   (19½ x 46½)
Collection of Mr. Derek FitzGerald, London, England

19

20. Fishermen and Birds   [undated]

grisaille on canvas   49.5 x 104.8   (19½ x 41½)
Collection of Mr. Derek FitzGerald, London, England

20

21. Capriccio View of the Dogana, Venice   [undated]

paper collage in plaster surround   43.8 x 66   (17¼ x 26)
Collection of The Hon. Charles Allsopp, London, England

21

22. The Forum, Rome, with Temple of Saturn

[undated]
watercolour and gouache   58.5 x 46   (23 x 18)
Private Collection

Notes: This is a study either for or after a panel of the same title in the Stoke Rochford series and now in the collection of Senor José M. Ortega Neyra, Madrid, Spain.

22

23. Mother Church in Italy   [undated]

oil on canvas   53.5 x 68.8   (21 x 27)
Collection of Dr. J. A. L. McCullough, McMurray, Pennsylvania

Notes: The original title of this painting and the identity of the church is uncertain. Based purely on titles in the Exhibition History, it may be the same as *Church Interior, Palma,* no. 51 in the 1949 Annan exhibition.

23

24. **Il Tempio e la Fontana, Rome** 1908
lithotint on paper 29.4 x 20.4 (11⅝ x 8)

25. **L'Obelisco, Piazza del Popolo, Rome** 1908
lithotint on paper 30.1 x 21.4 (11¾ x 8⅜)

26. **Piazza San Lorenzo, Florence** 1908
lithotint on paper 29.1 x 20.3 (11⅜ x 8)

27. **Bel San Giovanni, Florence** 1908
lithotint on paper 29.4 x 21.6 (11½ x 8½)

28. **Piazza San Firenze, Florence** 1908
lithotint on paper 29.6 x 18.3 (11⅝ x 7¼)

29. **San Giorgio Maggiore, Venice** 1908
lithotint on paper 29.1 x 18 (11⅜ x 7)

29

30. **San Geremia and Palazzo Labia, Venice** 1908
lithotint on paper 28.6 x 18.4 (11¼ x 7¼)

31. **Il Colleone and Piazza San Giovanni e Paolo, Venice,** 1908
lithotint on paper 29.4 x 21 (11½ x 8¼)

32. **Il Ponte, Scuola di San Marco, Venice** 1908
lithotint on paper 27.8 x 22.9 (10⅞ x 9)

30

33. **Randazzo, Sicily** 1908
lithotint on paper 29.5 x 18.1 (11⅝ x 7)

All of the above, from the collection of the National Gallery of Canada, Ottawa, will be shown in Guelph, Windsor and Toronto.

An identical series from the collections of the Art Gallery of Ontario, Toronto (Nos. 24, 25, 26, 28, 29, 30, 33), and Dr. Douglas Kerr-Lawson, Waterloo, Ontario (Nos. 27, 31, 32), will be shown in Burnaby, Calgary and Fredericton.

*Nos. 24, 28
Collection of the Art Gallery of Ontario
Gift from Sir Edmund Walker Collection, 1926*
*Nos. 25, 26, 29, 30, 33
Collection of the Art Gallery of Ontario
Gift from Mrs. W. H. Cawthra, 1944*

References: "The International Society's Ninth Exhibition," *International Studio* (London), April 1909, p. 132; "Studio Talk: London," *International Studio*, October 1912, pp. 312-16, repr. of *L'Obelisco;* Joseph Pennell, "The Senefelder Club and the Revival of Artistic Lithography," *The Studio*, February 1914, p. 5, repr. of *Il Ponte;* Joseph Pennell, *Cantor Lectures on Artistic Lithography*, pp. 45, 47; Hector Charlesworth, "The Pictures of J. Kerr-Lawson," *Saturday Night*, 20 June 1914, p. 4; Joseph Pennell, *Lithographers and Lithography*, p. 147, repr. of *Il Ponte;* Hector Charlesworth, "Studio Talk: Toronto," *The Studio*, May 1916, p. 274; Queen Mary to Caterina, 24 July and 8 August 1922, Lawson family archives.

Notes: These lithotints, "The Italian Set," are derived from ten of the Stoke Rochford mural panels. They were probably printed on the special Senefelder Club press and are the most widely distributed of Kerr-Lawson's print series. One of these, *San Geremia and Palazzo Labia, Venice,* has appeared several times in exhibition catalogues under the misnomer *San Geronimo.* The first occasion was as early as 1908, and the name persistently reappears in the Exhibition History.

32

24

26

28

25

27

31

33

34. **London Bridge**   ca. 1906-07
oil on canvas   139.7 x 124.46   (55 x 49)
Collection of Roger Gibbs, Esq., London, England

34

35. **St. Martin-in-the-Fields**   ca. 1906-07
oil on canvas   213.3 x 142.2   (84 x 56)
Collection of Roger Gibbs, Esq., London, England

35

36. **Horse Guards**   ca. 1906-07
oil on canvas   101.6 x 101.6   (40 x 40)
Collection of Roger Gibbs, Esq., London, England

References: Hector Charlesworth, "The Pictures of J. Kerr-Lawson," *Saturday Night,* 20 June 1914, p. 4, repr. of *St. Martin's . . .;* "Aldenham House, Hertfordshire, The Residence of The Hon. Vicary Gibbs," *Country Life,* 23 February 1924, pp. 286, 289, repr. of *London Bridge, Horse Guards* and *St. Martin's . . . .*

Notes: These three paintings were part of the series of London views commissioned by the first Lord Aldenham for the white parlour at Aldenham House, Hertfordshire, in 1906. A lithographed series was also made and another view of St. Martin's was turned into a poster for London Transport.

36

37. **St. Paul's Cathedral, London**   ca. 1906-11
oil on canvas   101.6 x 142.2   (40 x 56)
Collection of the National Gallery of Canada, Ottawa

References: "St. Paul's Cathedral, London," *The Canadian Magazine,* October 1918, p. 489, repr.; Robert H. Hubbard, *The National Gallery of Canada, Catalogue of Paintings and Sculptures, vol. II; Modern European Schools,* no. 319, p. 98, repr.

Notes: This is a slightly differing copy (in dimensions and foreground detail) of one of the Aldenham House panels. A small oil study for it is in the collection of Mrs. Madeleine Marx, London, England. Several lithographs of different sizes have also been made of the subject.

37

38. **London Bridge**   ca. 1908
lithograph on paper   63.5 x 55.9   (25 x 22)
Collection of Mr. B. Peter Hennessy, Vancouver B.C.

References: Malcolm C. Salaman, *Modern Woodcuts and Lithographs by British and French Artists,* pp. 123-24, 141, repr.

Notes: This is one of the series of lithographs after the Aldenham House panels.

38

39. **Joseph Pennell**   ca. 1908-09

lithograph on paper   32.3 x 21.5   (12¾ x 8½) (sheet)
Collection of the National Gallery of Canada, Ottawa

References: "Joseph Pennell," *Saturday Night,* 1 May 1926, p. 3, repr.; Elizabeth Robins Pennell, *The Life and Letters of Joseph Pennell,* p. 59.

Notes: Joseph Pennell (1860-1926) was a prominent American illustrator and printmaker, biographer of Whistler and friend of the Kerr-Lawsons. From 1884 to 1917, he and his wife Elizabeth were based in London. According to his wife, this was one of several lithographed portraits made of him during the winter of 1908-09. Other known copies are in the Art Gallery of Ontario and in the Print Room of the British Museum, London. An oil portrait of Pennell was in the 1948 Ferens Art Gallery exhibition (no. 44).

Will be shown in Guelph, Windsor and Toronto.

39

40. **William De Morgan**   1909

lithograph on paper   32 x 21.6   (12⅝ x 8½) (sheet)
Collection of the National Gallery of Canada, Ottawa

References: "William De Morgan," *Saturday Night,* 5 June 1926, p. 3, repr.

Notes: William Frend De Morgan (1839-1917) was a famous Pre-Raphaelite potter who, late in life, also became known as a novelist. He and his wife, the painter Evelyn De Morgan, lived in Chelsea and, after 1890, for part of each year in Florence. They knew the Kerr-Lawsons at least by 1895 and were dining with them in Chelsea when Heinemann dropped in to say that De Morgan's first novel, *Joseph Vance,* had just gone to the printers. This print is based on a 1908 pencil drawing in the National Portrait Gallery, London. Other known copies of the print are in the Art Gallery of Ontario and in the Print Room of the British Museum, London.

Will be shown in Guelph, Windsor and Toronto.

40

41. **James Havard Thomas**   [undated]

pencil on paper   33 x 25.4   (13 x 10)
Collection of the National Portrait Gallery, London, England

References: K. K. Yung, *National Portrait Gallery: Complete Illustrated Catalogue 1856-1979,* no. 2115, p. 565, repr.

Notes: James Havard Thomas (1854-1921) was a Paris trained portrait and figure sculptor and Professor of Sculpture at the Slade School, London. He worked in southern Italy for many years, having a villa on Capri. He was also a member of the International Society. A Kerr-Lawson pencil drawing of Thomas sleeping (Tate Gallery, London), is dated "Taormina, 26 March 1910," This drawing probably dates from about the same time.

41

42. **Maurice Hewlett**   ca. 1911

lithograph on paper   22.2 x 28.6   (8¾ x 11¼)
Collection of the Art Gallery of Ontario, Toronto, Ontario
Gift of Sir Edmund Walker Estate, 1926

Notes: This print is based on the 1904 oil portrait of Hewlett in the National Portrait Gallery, London (cat. no. 17). Another copy, in the collection of Dr. Douglas Kerr-Lawson, Waterloo, Ontario, is dated 1911.

42

43. **Theatre of Dionysus, Taormina, Sicily**   [undated]

oil on canvas   27.9 x 45.7   (11 x 18)
Collection of Dr. J. A. L. McCullough, McMurray, Pennsylvania

Notes: Taormina is a very picturesque Sicilian town with a large foreign colony. Many artists have lived or visited there. Kerr-Lawson visited there in 1910 and 1912 and probably came back a number of times. He painted many works there, most now unlocated. Other Taormina works are with Dr. Douglas Kerr-Lawson and Mrs. Peter F. Groff. A watercolour titled *Greek Theatre, Taormina* was included in the 1948 Beaux Arts Gallery Memorial exhibition (no. 49) and in the Annan exhibition of 1949 (no. 5).

43

44

44. **Taormina Street Scene** [undated]
oil 19 x 29.3 (7½ x 11½)
Collection of Dr. J. A. L. McCullough, McMurray, Pennsylvania

45

45. **Florence, Showing the Bridges Spanning the Arno** [undated]
oil on canvas 31.7 x 41.9 (12½ x 16½)
Collection of Her Majesty Queen Elizabeth II, Windsor Castle, Berkshire, England

Notes: This is probably the painting given to Her Majesty Queen Mary in 1925. The Queen and her parents had lived in Florence from 1883 to 1885, and in a letter to Mrs. Kerr-Lawson (8 May 1925) she mentioned that the painting served as a "pleasant reminder" of those days.

46

46. **Winter in Kent** ca. 1912-13
lithograph on paper 24.1 x 34.3 (9½ x 13½)
Collection of Dr. Dorothy J. McCullough, Toronto, Ontario

References: "Fine Pictures at the Canadian Art Club Show," *The Globe* (Toronto), 10 May 1913; "Winter in Kent," *Colour*, December 1922 - January 1923, p. 100, repr.; "London News and Comment: Kerr-Lawson Pictures," *The Scotsman* (Edinburgh), 5 November 1942; "Art Exhibitions," *The Times* (London), 11 November 1942; T. W. Earp, "Artist Who Did Not Exhibit: Posthumous Show," *The Daily Telegraph* (London), 17 November 1942.

Notes: In the years just before World War I, Kerr-Lawson painted a number of Kentish subjects. This lithograph is based on a notable oil of this period first exhibited at the Canadian Art Club in 1913 (no. 57) and then at the Beaux Arts Gallery in 1942 and the Institut Français d'Ecosse in 1952 (no. 19). In 1952 it was part of the Waite Collection but it is now unlocated. A closely related watercolour, *Near Sandwich,* is now in the Johannesburg Art Gallery, Johannesburg, South Africa.

47

47. **Farm Labourer at Northbourne, Kent** [undated]
oil on panel 40 x 23.8 (15¾ x 9⅜)
Collection of Dr. Dorothy J. McCullough, Toronto, Ontario

Notes: This is another of the pre-war Kentish subjects. Six of them were included in the Twenty-One Gallery exhibition of 1914.

48

48. **Harvesting** [undated]
oil on panel 20.4 x 34.7 (8 x 13⅝)
Collection of Mr. and Mrs. Jules Loeb, Toronto, Ontario

Notes: This is probably another Kentish scene.

49

49. **Easton Grey** [undated]
lithograph on paper 18 x 25.1 (7 x 9⅞)
Collection of Dr. Dorothy J. McCullough, Toronto, Ontario

50. **English Pastoral Scene with House, Trees and Pool** [undated]
lithograph on paper   20.9 x 23.5   (8¼ x 9¼)
Collection of Dr. Dorothy J. McCullough, Toronto, Ontario

Notes: Kerr-Lawson is supposed to have done a number of lithographs of English subjects (aside from the Aldenham House subjects) though whether these are part of a formal series is unknown. Three of them were exhibited with the Canadian Art Club in 1915 but no further record of exhibitions exists. These two lithographs, in theme and mood, are similar to the works of George Clausen, from the decade before World War I. Other known English subjects are *Boston, Stratford-on-Avon, Windmill in Kent* and *Tattersal Castle.*

50

51. **Boston, Lincolnshire**   1913
oil on canvas   99 x 137.2   (39 x 54)
Collection of Dr. J. A. L. McCullough, McMurray, Pennsylvania

References: Canadian Art Club, 1913, repr. in catalogue; "Fine Pictures at the Canadian Art Club Show," *The Globe* (Toronto), 10 May 1913; Lawren S. Harris, "Canadian Art Club," in *The Year Book of Canadian Art 1913,* p. 214.

Notes: St. Botolph's Church, is one of the largest English parish churches in the Gothic style. Kerr-Lawson may have painted it while visiting Stoke Rochford Hall, also in Lincolnshire. An oil sketch for the painting is in the Ferens Art Gallery, Hull, England. A lithograph after it is with Mr. B. Peter Hennessy, Vancouver, B.C.

51

52. **Boston, Lincolnshire**   ca. 1913-15
lithograph on paper   50.8 x 71.1   (20 x 28)
Collection of Mr. B. Peter Hennessy, Vancouver, B.C.

52

53. **Sir John Lavery, R.A.**   ca. 1913
oil on canvas   43.8 x 33.6   (17¼ x 13¼)
Collection of the Ferens Art Gallery, Kingston upon Hull, England
Gift of Mrs. James Kerr-Lawson, 1948

Notes: Sir John Lavery (1856-1941) was a noted portrait and landscape painter. Like Kerr-Lawson, he had studied at the Académie Julian, was a member of the Glasgow School and often worked in Tangier. Moving to London during the 1890s, he organized the International Society and began a career as a fashionable portraitist. Here he is shown painting *The Royal Family at Buckingham Palace* (1913), now in the National Portrait Gallery, London. The portrait bears the inscription "GIO. LAVERY, PITTORE OTTIMO, UOMO AMABILISSIMO" and was included in the 1952 Institut Français d'Ecosse exhibition (no. 12). A pencil drawing for it is in the Scottish National Portrait Gallery, Edinburgh (cat. no. 1436).

53

54. **Spanish Beggar**   [undated]
oil   36.8 x 20.3   (14½ x 8)
Collection of Dr. J. A. L. McCullough, McMurray, Pennsylvania

Notes: This may be the same as no. 7 or no. 12 in the 1914 Twenty-One Gallery exhibition. A lithograph in "The Spanish Set" also bears this title.

54

55. Gypsy Water Carrier, Cordova [undated]
oil   38.2 x 25.5   (15 x 10)
Collection of Dr. J. A. L. McCullough, McMurray, Pennsylvania

Notes: This is probably the same as no. 31 in the 1914 Twenty-One Gallery exhibition, no. 19 in the 1948 Heffer Gallery exhibition, no. 49 in the 1949 Annan exhibition, no. 22 in the 1948 Ferens Art Gallery exhibition and no. 95 in the 1952 Institut Français d'Ecosse exhibition. A lithograph in "The Spanish Set" also bears this title.

55

56. Cordova [undated]
oil on canvas   24.2 x 33.1   (9½ x 13)
Collection of Mrs. Keith Thomson, North Vancouver, B.C.

56

57. A Moorish Market   ca. 1913-14
oil on canvas   48.5 x 53.5   (19 x 21)
Collection of FORBES Magazine, New York

References: Canadian National Exhibition, 1914, no. 55 (as *Shopping in Morocco*), repr. in catalogue; "A Moorish Market," *Colour,* December 1921, p. 98, repr.; *Sotheby's at Scone Palace, Perthshire,* 24 April 1979, lot 549, p. 127, repr.

Notes: One of Kerr-Lawson's finest Moroccan scenes, this may well be the same painting exhibited at the Grosvenor Galleries *Colour Magazine Exhibition of Modern Art,* March-April 1922, no. 21, for sale £75 or the work sold to Smith at Christie's on 30 November 1934, lot 169. A lithograph, possibly related to it, and titled either *Shopping* or *Shopping in Tetuan* was included in the 1913 and 1914 Twenty-One Gallery exhibitions.

57

58. St. Martin-in-the-Fields   1913
lithographed poster   101.6 x 63.5   (40 x 25) (sheet)
Collection of Dr. J. A. L. McCullough, McMurray, Pennsylvania

Notes: This is one of two Kerr-Lawson posters done for London Transport, the other being *Westminster Abbey, Broad Sanctuary,* printed in August 1915. Though based on the same subject as one of the Aldenham House panels, this poster shows a view further from the south, across Trafalgar Square. A copy of the lithograph on which it was based was sold to Queen Mary in 1922. Another lithographed view of St. Martin's is in the National Gallery of Canada, Ottawa.

58

59. Westminster Abbey and St. Margaret's Church
[undated]
lithograph on paper   31.1 x 34.4   (12¼ x 13½)
Collection of Mr. B. Peter Hennessy, Vancouver, B.C.

Notes: This lithograph, though based on London monuments, does not relate to the existing Aldenham House panels. It was later adapted for a London Transport poster, *Sightseeing: Westminster Abbey, Broad Sanctuary,* printed in August, 1915. Copies of the poster are now with London Transport and in the Print Room of the British Museum.

59

60. **"This England never did, nor never shall, Lie at the proud foot of a conqueror."** — *Shakespeare*

ca. 1914-15

lithographed recruiting poster   67 x 46   (26⅜ x 18)

Collection of the University of Guelph, Macdonald Stewart Art Centre, Guelph, Ontario

Gift of Norah McCullough, 1979

References: Judith M. Nasby, *The University of Guelph Art Collection,* no. 79.10, p. 194.

Notes: This is probably one of the recruiting posters made by members of the Senefelder Club for the London Underground.

60

61. **"What I Gave I Have"**   ca. 1916

lithograph on paper   45 x 35.7   (17⅝ x 14⅞)

Collection of the University of Guelph, Macdonald Stewart Art Centre, Guelph, Ontario

Gift of Norah McCullough, 1979

References: "What I Gave I Have," *Saturday Night,* 5 August 1916, p. 11, repr.; Judith M. Nasby, *The University of Guelph Art Collection,* no. 79.9, p. 194, repr.

Notes: This is a print for a commemorative stamp to be sold for the benefit of the British Red Cross Fund.

61

62. **The Cloth Hall, Ypres**   ca. 1917-18

oil on canvas   71.2 x 19.5   (28 x 36)

Collection of Mr. Thomas P. Kohn-Speyer, Hailsham, East Sussex, England

63. **Arras Cathedral**   ca. 1917-18

oil on canvas   71.2 x 19.5   (28 x 36)

Collection of Mr. Thomas P. Kohn-Speyer, Hailsham, East Sussex, England

Notes: These two works are highly finished studies for or after Kerr-Lawson's two large murals, done for the Canadian War Records Office and now in the Senate, Parliament Hill, Ottawa.

64. **Anstruther Abercrombie Lawson**   8 March 1920

pencil on paper   36.8 x 37.5   (14⅜ x 14¾)

Collection of the University of Guelph, Macdonald Stewart Art Centre, Guelph, Ontario

Gift of Dr. Dorothy J. McCullough and Norah McCullough, 1974

References: "Prof. A. A. Lawson," *Saturday Night,* 9 September 1922, repr.; Francis E. Vaughan, *Andrew C. Lawson,* p. 39; Judith M. Nasby, *The University of Guelph Art Collection,* no. 74.16, p. 193, repr.

Notes: Anstruther Abercrombie Lawson (1870-1926), Kerr-Lawson's younger brother, taught at Stanford and the University of Glasgow and eventually became Professor of Botany at the University of Sydney, Australia. He was also a minor art collector who consulted his brother on his purchases. It was he who discovered in New Zealand the *Christ Crowned with Thorns* attributed to Bosch (now with Dr. J. A. L. McCullough). This drawing is one of several studies for a 1922 oil portrait at the University of Sydney. Other studies, more closely related to the portrait, are with the University of Guelph and Dr. J. A. L. McCullough. An earlier charcoal drawing of A. A. Lawson was exhibited at the 1908 International Society (no. 357).

64

65. **The Annunciation** ca. 1924
paper mosaic on paper 218.4 x 157.5 (86 x 62)
Collection of the Art Gallery of Ontario, Toronto, Ontario
Gift of W. H. Cawthra and the Artist, 1926
Shown in Toronto only.

References: A. S. Hartrick, "James Kerr-Lawson's Decorative Panels,"
Saturday Night, 19 June 1926, p. 5, repr.; "Famous Artist," *Saturday
Night,* 30 July 1926; " 'The Annunciation' Decorative Panel by J.
Kerr-Lawson," *The Studio,* October 1926, pp. 275, 278-79, repr.;
Frederick Lessore, "The Decorative Paintings of James Kerr-Lawson,"
The Studio, January 1927, pp. 26-28; Herbert Furst, "The Adoration
of the Shepherds: A Paper Mosaic by J. Kerr-Lawson," *Apollo,*
October 1927, pp. 183-85, repr.

Notes: This is one of the two decorative panels done for the chapel in
the Palace of Arts of the British Empire Exhibition at Wembley. Its
companion piece, *The Adoration of the Shepherds,* was once in the
Ferens Art Gallery, Hull, England, but is now unlocated. A study for it
is included in the exhibition (cat. no. 66).

65

66. **Study for "Adoration of the Shepherds"** ca. 1924
oil on panel 63.5 x 56 (25 x 22)
Collection of Leslie Maddock Lash, White Plains, N.Y.

67. **Self-Portrait** ca. 1926
pencil on paper 23.5 x 16.5 (9¼ x 6½)
Collection of Dr. J. A. L. McCullough, McMurray, Pennsylvania

Notes: This drawing was included in the 1926 Beaux Arts Gallery
exhibition. The signature placed in the cigar smoke is a conceit typical
in Kerr-Lawson's later works. A lithograph based on it was reproduced
in *Saturday Night,* 8 May 1926, p. 3, and in *Apollo,* June 1939, p.
311.

66

67

68. **Andrew Cowper Lawson** ca. 1929-30
oil on canvas 127.6 x 101.9 (50¼ x 40⅛)
Collection of the University Art Museum, University of
California, Berkeley, California
Andrew C. Lawson Bequest

References: "Prof. Andrew C. Lawson," *Saturday Night,* 8 May 1926,
p. 3, repr.; *Saturday Night,* 12 April 1930, p. 13, repr.; Francis E.
Vaughan, *Andrew C. Lawson,* pp. 34, 223.

Notes: Andrew C. Lawson (1861-1952), Kerr-Lawson's older brother,
was a famous geologist and seismologist and, for many years, head of
the geology department of the University of California at Berkeley.
His profession is referred to in the inscription "Terram Trementem/
Montes Fumantes." A pencil drawing for the portrait was reproduced
in 1926 in *Saturday Night* and is now with Dr. J. A. L. McCullough.

68

69. **Cheyne Walk, Carlyle's Statue,
Cheyne Row and Archdeacon Bevan** [undated]
oil on canvas 195 x 136 (76¾ x 53½)
Collection of the Royal Borough of Kensington and Chelsea,
Chelsea Library, London, England
Gift of Mrs. James Kerr-Lawson, 1942

References: "Gift to Chelsea Library," *West London Press,* 18
September 1942.

Notes: The scene depicted was close to Kerr-Lawson's Chelsea
studio. Thomas Carlyle, whose statue by Sir Edgar Boehm is shown,
long lived on Cheyne Row, the street going off to the left. The Rev.
Henry E. J. Bevan (1854-1935) was Archdeacon of Middlesex and
Rector of St. Luke's parish church in Chelsea from 1902 to 1930.

69

70. **Market Scene with Four Figures** [late 1920s]
colour lithograph on paper with fabric backing
96.9 x 146.7 (38⅛ x 57¾)

70

71. **"The People Bring Much More than Enough for the Service of the Work"**—*Exodus 36:5* [late 1920s]
colour lithograph on paper with fabric backing
97.3 x 146.4 (38¼ x 57⅝)

71

72. **"...And at Our Gates Are All Manner of Pleasant Fruits, New and Old"** — *Song of Solomon 7:13*
[late 1920s]
colour lithograph on paper with fabric backing
97.3 x 146.8 (38¼ x 57¾)
Collection of the University of Guelph, Macdonald Stewart Art Centre, Guelph, Ontario
All of the above: Gift of Norah McCullough, 1979

References: Judith M. Nasby, *The University of Guelph Art Collection,* no. 79.11.3, 79.11.5 and 79.11.6, pp. 194-95, repr.

Notes: These are probably proofs (three of six) for a lithographed poster designed for the Empire Marketing Board. During the twenties and early thirties, the Board commissioned posters from many artists to promote free trade within the British Empire. Some of these, though not Kerr-Lawson's were exhibited at the Royal Academy in November 1926 and were often mentioned in *The Times.* Many of the figures in the frieze are taken from two grisaille paintings originally part of the Stoke Rochford murals. These were sold at Christie's, 21 July 1978, lot 66, and are now with Waldheim Old Master Paintings, Hambledon, Hampshire, England. An unidentified newspaper clipping with Mrs. Peter F. Groff shows a framed, five panel series identified as the Marketing Board poster. Only two of the panels relate to the Guelph and Stoke Rochford images. A watercolour for one of the five, *Peace Calling on Sea,* is also with Mrs. Groff.

72

73. **Segovia** ca. 1929-30
oil on canvas 63.5 x 75 (25 x 29½)
Collection of Mr. K. Y. Alghanim, Windsor, England

Notes: The Kerr-Lawsons travelled in Morocco and Spain in 1929. Two views of Segovia dating from about this time are in the Alghanim Collection. Another similar view was included in the Beaux Arts Gallery exhibition in 1930 (no. 22), and reproduced in *The Illustrated London News,* 25 October 1930, p. 716. This painting was probably in the 1952 Institut Français d'Ecosse exhibition (no. 29).

73

74. **Unknown Spanish Castle** [undated]
tempera on canvas 26.3 x 36.2 (10⅜ x 14¼)
Collection of Dr. Dorothy J. McCullough, Toronto, Ontario

Notes: This is probably one of the Spanish subjects either in the 1914 Twenty-One Gallery exhibition or in the 1930 Beaux Arts Gallery exhibition.

74

75. The Dream of Morocco [late 1920s]

oil on canvas 67.9 x 72.5 (26¾ x 28½)

Collection of the National Gallery of Canada, Ottawa
Gift of Mrs. James Kerr-Lawson, 1948

References: "The Dream," *Saturday Night,* 13 December 1930, p. 1, repr.; Kineton Parkes, "Kerr-Lawson at the Beaux Arts Gallery," *Apollo,* November 1930, p. 368, repr.; Hector Charlesworth, "James Kerr-Lawson," *Canadian Home Journal,* February 1931, pp. 18, 55, repr.; *Montreal Gazette,* 1 September 1943; Robert H. Hubbard, *The National Gallery of Canada, Catalogue of Paintings and Sculptures, Vol. II: Modern European Schools,* no. 6063, p. 209.

Notes: A nearly identical version of this work is in the Alghanim Collection. On the back it bears the inscription "Pierre Johns-'Maroco'/The Easte bowed low before the blast,/In patient deep disdain/She let the legions thunder past,/Then plunged in thought again./ Matthew Arnold's 'Oberman Once More' ". The inclusion of the exotic bird may show the influence of Frank Brangwyn and his many drawings, about this time, for his British Empire Panels in the House of Lords.

75

76

76. Grenadine Lady ca. 1930

oil on canvas 63.5 x 50.8 (25 x 20)

Collection of Leslie Maddock Lash, White Plains, N.Y.

References: Kineton Parkes, "Kerr-Lawson at the Beaux Arts Gallery," *Apollo,* November 1930, p. 368, repr.

Notes: This work was in the 1930 Beaux Arts Gallery exhibition (no. 7). The identity of the sitter is unknown and the background is similar to that in the *Portrait of Mrs. W. H. Cawthra* (cat. no. 79).

77

77. Sir Frank Brangwyn in Moorish Dress ca. 1926-31

tempera on board 38.2 x 30.6 (15 x 12)

Collection of Mr. K. Y. Alghanim, Windsor, England

References: "A Famous Royal Academician as a Moorish Chief: Mr. Frank Brangwyn," *The Illustrated London News,* 10 October 1934, repr.

Notes: See notes on Kerr-Lawson's 1936 Brangwyn portrait (cat. no. 81). This portrait, formerly in the Waite collection, was included in the 1942 Beaux Arts Gallery exhibition and was no. 14 in the 1952 Institut Français d'Ecosse exhibition.

78

78. Portrait of Paul Henry Kohn-Speyer ca. 1930

oil on canvas 91.5 x 71.2 (36 x 28)

Collection of Mr. and Mrs. Edmund Paul Speyer, Tenby, S. Wales

Notes: Paul Henry Kohn-Speyer (died ca. 1942), member of a famous British financial family, was a partner in the London firm of Brandeis Goldschmidt and Co. Ltd., metal traders. About the turn of the century he became a close friend of Kerr-Lawson. Note the characteristic Kerr-Lawson self-portrait reflected in Kohn-Speyer's pince-nez, and the table-top statuette used later in *Fortune* (cat. no. 82).

79. **Portrait of Mrs. W. H. Cawthra** ca. 1931

oil on canvas 76.1 x 62.2 (29⅞ x 24½)
Collection of the National Gallery of Canada, Ottawa
Gift of the Cawthra Estate, 1957

References: "Portrait of Mrs. W. H. Cawthra," *Saturday Night,* 22 August 1931, p. 11, repr.; Robert H. Hubbard, *The National Gallery of Canada, Catalogue of Paintings and Sculptures, vol. II: Modern European Schools,* no. 6769, p. 98, repr.

Notes: Anne Maude Cawthra (nee Beatty) married William Herbert (Bertie) Cawthra in Toronto in 1897 and died there in the mid 1950s. Scion of an old Toronto family, Cawthra, a man of private means, travelled extensively and was a minor patron and collector of art. He and his wife probably knew the Kerr-Lawsons from their interest in the Canadian Art Club and from their frequent travels to London. In 1926 and 1944, they gave a number of Kerr-Lawson's works to the Art Gallery of Toronto. This portrait is typical of Kerr-Lawson's late works. Mrs. Cawthra's nephew, the architect Anthony Adamson, O.C., remembers it as "the rather frightening portrait of Maude Cawthra. It was a spitting likeness."

79

80. **Portrait of Homer Watson** ca. 1930s

lithograph on paper 40.3 x 30.1 (15⅞ x 11¾)
Collection of the National Gallery of Canada, Ottawa

Notes: Homer Ransford Watson (1855-1936), the Canadian painter, was a relative by marriage and life-long friend of Kerr-Lawson who had painted a portrait of him in Pittenweem in 1888. It was once with Mrs. Ross Hamilton in Doon, Ontario, and is now unlocated. From Watson's appearance, this lithographed portrait must date from his final years. The circumstances in which it was made are unknown.

Exhibited in Guelph, Windsor and Toronto.

80

81. **Sir Frank Brangwyn** 1936

oil on canvas 99 x 78.7 (39 x 31)
Collection of the Ferens Art Gallery, Kingston upon Hull, England

References: "Donor of his Works to Bruges and Honoured as her 'Glorious Son'," *The Illustrated London News,* 8 August 1936, p. 247, repr.; "Portrait of Frank Brangwyn," *The Times* (London), 14 August 1936, repr.; *Catalogue of Works by Frank Brangwyn, R.A., LL.D. in the Permanent Collection,* Ferens Art Gallery, Hull, 1936, p. 44, frontispiece.

Notes: Sir Frank Brangwyn (1867-1956) was a noted British mural painter, printmaker and designer. He and Kerr-Lawson were old friends, were both members of the Senefelder Club and worked together on the 1922 Venice Biennale. They also wrote tributes to one another, Kerr-Lawson for Brangwyn's 1924 Queen's Gate exhibition and Brangwyn for Kerr-Lawson's obituary in *The Studio.* In addition to the two portraits of Brangwyn in this exhibition, there is also a portrait drawing in the Print Room of the British Museum, London. This portrait bears two inscriptions testifying to the friendship between the two men. One is an adaptation of a Montaigne saying, "Parce que c'estoit lui, parce que c'estoit moy". The other "Io piccolo; lui grande" is inscribed by Kerr-Lawson's head on the medallion in Brangwyn's right hand. The exotic birds and flowers in the background refer to Brangwyn's love of oriental art and to his British Empire Panels for the House of Lords.

81

82. **Fortune** [late 1930s]

oil on canvas 64.7 x 96.5 (25½ x 38)

Collection of Mr. K. Y. Alghanim, Windsor, England

References: "Mr. J. Kerr-Lawson: Funeral of Famous Artist," *West London Press,* 12 May 1939; Frank Brangwyn, "Obituary: J. Kerr-Lawson," *The Studio,* July 1939, p. 33; unedited typescript of Brangwyn obituary, collection of Leslie Maddock Lash, White Plains, N.Y.; Adrian Bury, *Two Centuries of British Water-Colour Painting,* p. 168; foreword to catalogue of 1952 Institut Français d'Ecosse exhibition.

Notes: These are probably two of five panels finished for the Waites in White Lodge, Hampstead. Some of the five panels are supposed to have been oval. These ones were included in the 1952 Institut Français d'Ecosse exhibition (nos. 22 and 28). Another work from the series, *The Water Wheel,* is also in the Alghanim Collection. Some of the motifs in *The Mirage* are taken from two of the Stoke Rochford grisaille panels (now with Waldheim Old Master Paintings) and from *A Moorish Market.* The back of *Fortune* bears an inscription from Dante's *Inferno* (canto 7, line 68) "Questa Fortuna, di che tu mi tocche." The statue in the painting is a pastiche of Bernardo Falcone's *Fortuna,* atop the Dogana da Mar in Venice, and Pietro Tacca's four slaves in chains at the base of the *Monument to the Grand Duke Ferdinand I of Tuscany* in Livorno. It appears as a table top statuette in Kerr-Lawson's portrait of his friend Paul Kohn-Speyer (cat. no. 78).

82

83. **Portrait of Bernard Berenson** ca. 1938-39

tempera on board 38 x 26.8 (15 x 10½)

Collection of Mrs. Barbara Halpern, Oxford, England

Notes: Bernard Berenson (1865-1959) was the leading expert of his day on Italian Renaissance art. A Lithuanian Jew, he was raised in Boston and graduated from Harvard but spent most of his life as an expatriate in Florence. He made a fortune from advising the dealer Duveen, and various American collectors. About April 1897, he and his wife Mary sat to Kerr-Lawson for portrait drawings. The drawing of Berenson is now in the Berenson Archive and that of Mary is unlocated. During the late thirties, Berenson lent Kerr-Lawson his portrait drawing to make a painted version of it. Kerr-Lawson was working on this version up until his death. He also exhibited a view of Berenson's villa, I Tatti, in his Dowdeswell Galleries exhibition (no. 17).

83

51 Boston, Lincolnshire 1913

6   *La Caterina   ca. 1887*

Catalogue number, title, medium, lender and price will be listed in that order when available.
(Full data is seldom given in the original catalogues.)

1882

Royal Canadian Academy of Arts Third Annual Exhibition, Montreal

12.	Twilight in Italy	oil	$100
61.	An old Roman building	oil	58
65.	Study in Rome	oil	50
85.	Bay of Naples	oil	50

1883

Royal Canadian Academy of Arts and Ontario Society of Artists Exhibition, Toronto

8.	The Cactus Bower	oil	$100
14.	A Capri landscape	oil	100
93.	Winnowing	oil	100

Art Association of Montreal Annual Spring Exhibition, Montreal

80.	Winnowing	oil
109.	The Cactus Bower, Capri	oil
130.	A Capri Landscape (twilight)	oil

1885

Royal Canadian Academy of Arts and Ontario Society of Artists Exhibition, Toronto

31.	Village Green, Runswick, England	oil	$75
35.	Piping Pan	oil	75
73.	Twilight	oil	75
76.	After the Carnival	oil	75

Ontario Society of Artists Winter Exhibition, Toronto

14.	The Orphans	oil
18.	Portrait—Fannie	oil
19.	The Lane	oil
32.	Garden Path	oil
35.	"Music, when soft voices die, Vibrates in the memory."	oil
40.	Portrait of a Lady	oil
58.	A Colloquy	oil
87.	Sketch from life	watercolour
88.	Landscape	watercolour
90.	The Lane	watercolour

Art Association of Montreal Spring Exhibition, Montreal

3.	After the Carnival	oil
14.	An old Fisherman	oil
60.	Twilight	oil
69.	Village Green, Runswick, England	oil
75.	Piping Pan	oil

1886

Royal Canadian Academy of Arts Seventh Annual Exhibition, Ottawa

1.	Twilight	oil	$50
42.	Sketch	watercolour	15
130.	"Music, when soft voices die, Vibrates in the memory." Shelley	oil	
136.	The Orphans	oil	$150
171.	A Colloquy	oil	
181.	After the Carnival	oil	75
185.	Portrait—James Smith, Treas. RCA	oil	

Ontario Society of Artists Fourteenth Annual Exhibition, Toronto

51.	At the Window	oil	$40
69.	Portrait	oil	
72.	Portrait	oil	

Art Association of Montreal, Montreal

Hoeing Potatoes

1887

Rembrandt Art Rooms, Toronto

[Painting of a girl at a piano]

W. Scott and Son Twelfth Annual Sale, Montreal, 23 April

43.	Study (Head of a Sailor)	oil	
46.	Winter	oil	$25

Rembrandt Art Rooms, Toronto

[Study of a head and two other works]

1888

Art Association of Montreal Annual Spring Exhibition

9.	Jacques Bonhomme	oil	$150

1889

Ontario Society of Artists Seventeenth Annual Exhibition, Toronto

19.	The Snuff Taker	oil	$200
45.	Scene in Tangier, Morocco	oil	75

Royal Canadian Academy of Arts Tenth Annual Exhibition, Ottawa

2.	Market Scene, Tangier, Morocco	oil	$25
3.	Market Scene, Tangier, Morocco	oil	25

4.	Street Scene, Tangier, Morocco *oil*	25
12.	Hazy Day on the Mediterranean *oil*	25
13.	Mediterranean Coast, Morocco *oil*	25
16.	Summer Landscape, Southern France *oil*	40
34.	A Moorish Landscape *oil*	30
78.	A Moorish Court *oil*	25
82.	At Brolles, Fontainebleau *oil*	

1890

Royal Glasgow Institute of Fine Arts, Glasgow

520.	The Potato Harvest in Fife *oil*	£105

Royal Society of British Artists, London

402.	Rigging the Model	£60

1891

Toronto Industrial Exhibition, Toronto

143.	June *oil* *A. Jardine Esq.*	

1892

Royal Glasgow Institute of Fine Arts, Glasgow

61.	A study *oil*	£15.15
195.	Moorish Cavalry *oil*	£15.15

1893

Royal Glasgow Institute of Fine Arts, Glasgow

681.	The Ploughman *oil*	£60

4   Portrait of James Smith   ca. 1886

51

1896

Society of Portrait Painters, London

82. Portrait of a Gentleman

1897

Royal Glasgow Institute of Fine Arts, Glasgow

586. Portrait of D. McCorkindale, Esq. *oil*

1898

Toronto Industrial Exhibition, Toronto

285. A Country Road *oil*

Royal Glasgow Institute of Fine Arts, Glasgow

36. Venice Seascape *oil*   £40
606. San Juan de Dios, Granada

International Society of Sculptors, Painters and Gravers, London

278. Venice *oil*

1899

International Society of Sculptors, Painters and Gravers, London

147. Portrait of Cecco—son of Maurice Hewlett, Esq. *oil*

Womens Art Association, Portrait Exhibition, Toronto

292. Henry James Grasett, D.D. 1886 *Dr. F. LeM. Grasett*
370. Dean Grasett *Dr. F. LeM. Grasett*

[Possible summer exhibition in George Watts' studio, London.]

1903

The Dowdeswell Galleries, London

Little Landscapes of Italy by J. Kerr-Lawson   April

1. Venice
2. Bergamo
3. Santa Maria Novella
4. The Arno, Florence
5. Montesca
6. The Ramparts, Lucca
7. The Gate, Pisa
8. The Zattere, Venice
9. Madrugada
10. Via dei Servi, Florence
11. Dogana, Venice
12. Viale Principe Amedeo, Florence
13. San Lorenzo, Florence
14. Tiber at Città di Castello
15. The Tower, Pisa
16. San Giorgio, Venice
17. I Tatti, near Settignano
18. The Piazza, Siena
19. Ponte-a-Sieve
20. The Loggia, Casa di Boccaccio
21. Venice
22. San Juan di Dios, Granada
23. The Arno at Pisa
24. The Cathedral from S. Domenico, Siena
25. Piazza of Città di Castello
26. Salute, Venice
27. Gate at Città di Castello
28. Montepulciano
29. The Darro, Granada
30. Scirocco, Città di Castello
31. Torcello
32. Borgo Pace, in Umbria
33. L'Osservanza, Siena
34. Florence from the Piazzale
35. Vallombrosa from Rovezzano
36. San Martino à Mensola
37. The Riva, Venice
38. Certaldo
39. The Ferry, Rovezzano
40. Venice

Canadian National Exhibition, Toronto

89. The Cactus Bower, Capri *oil* *J. Massey*
90. Old Man *oil*

1904

International Society of Sculptors, Painters and Gravers, London

[copy of catalogue unlocated]

Dusseldorf International Exhibition, Dusseldorf

2065. Portrait of a Man (Henry James Ross)

Canadian National Exhibition, Toronto

41. Garth Street Road, Hamilton *oil* *Mrs. H. Martin*

1905

International Society of Sculptors, Painters and Gravers, London

155. Italian Village *wc*
156. The Square Tower *wc*
393. Italian Market *wc*
394. An Italian Port *wc*
398. Italian Hill Town *wc*
431. The Gateway *wc*

22　The Forum, Rome, with Temple of Saturn　[undated]

1906

The Alpine Club Gallery, London

J. Kerr-Lawson's Decorations for the Drawing Room at Stoke Rochford, Grantham
8 June-27 July

1. Forum
2. Temple of Vesta
3. Arch of Titus
4. San Firenze
5. Fivizzano
6. Palazzo Labia
7. Colleone
8. Piazza del Popolo
9. Randazzo
10. Pistoja
11. Baptistry, Florence
12. San Lorenzo

1907

Canadian National Exhibition, Toronto

79. A Roadway   *C. W. Irwin, Toronto*
90. The Boatmaker   *Elizabeth Lawson, Toronto*

1908

International Society of Sculptors, Painters and Gravers, London

26. Temple of Vesta   *lithotint*
357. Portrait of Dr. A. A. Lawson   *charcoal drawing*

The Dowdeswell Galleries, London

Lithotints by J. Kerr-Lawson: The Italian Set
December

81. San Geronimo
82. Colleone
83. Il Ponte
84. Randazzo
85. Bel San Giovanni
86. San Firenze
87. L'Obelisco
88. San Giorgio
89. Il Tempio e la Fontana
90. San Lorenzo

1909

International Society of Sculptors, Painters and Gravers, London

47-56 Italian Set   *lithotints*

47. Colleone
48. L'Obelisco
49. Bel San Giovanni
50. San Geronimo
51. San Giorgio
52. Il Ponte

53. Randazzo
54. San Lorenzo
55. San Firenze
56. Il Tempio e la Fontana
444. William de Morgan, Esq.   *drawing*

1911

Walker Art Gallery, Liverpool. Liverpool Autumn Exhibition

Senefelder Club section   lithotints each 3 guineas

1323. St. Mark's
1324. L'Obelisco
1325. Randazzo
1326. San Lorenzo
1327. Il Colleone, Venice
1328. Il Tempio e la Fontana
1329. The Tower and the Dome
1330. Il Ponte

1912

Canadian Art Club, Toronto, Fifth Annual Exhibition   8-27 February

41. Aci Reale
42. Santa Venere
43. San Pancrazio
44. Lidda
45. Piazza Cappucini

Art Museum of Toronto Fifth Loan Exhibition 11 April - 11 May

775. Portrait of Joseph Pennell   *lithograph*
     Sir Edmund Walker

"The Italian Set"   *lithographs   Sir Edmund Walker*

776. San Geronimo
777. Colleone
778. Il Ponte
779. Randazzo
780. Bel San Giovanni
781. San Firenze
782. Il Tempio e la Fontana
783. San Lorenzo
784. L'Obelisco
785. San Giorgio
786. Portrait of Maurice Hewlett   *lithograph   Miss Lawson*
787. Portrait of William de Morgan   *lithograph   Miss Lawson*

Venice Biennale

(rooms B and C devoted to Senefelder Club)

61. Randazzo
62. San Giorgio
63. Colleone
64. Il Ponte
65. San Geronimo
66. L'Obelisco
67. Il Tempio e la Fontana
68. San Giovanni

17   Maurice Henry Hewlett   1904

1913

Canadian Art Club, Toronto, Sixth Annual Exhibition   9 May - 31 May

56.   Boston   *oil*
57.   Winter in Kent   *oil*

Twenty-One Gallery, London

Lithographs by C. H. Shannon, J. Pennell,
J. Kerr-Lawson, Wm. Shackleton, Cecil French,
E. Gabian, L. Jacobs   6 June - 10 July

1.	Shopping	£3.3
2.	The Blacksmith	£3.3
13.	The Fondak	£3.3

Canadian National Exhibition, Toronto

37.	El Hadaddy, Morocco *oil*	$300
315.	Boston, Lincolnshire *oil*	

1914

Twenty-One Gallery, London

Paintings by J. Kerr-Lawson and Etchings by
Edgar Wilson   16 April - 11 June

1.	Sandwich, Kent	10 gns.
2.	Sandwich, Kent	10 gns.
3.	Sandwich, Kent	7 gns.
4.	Sandwich, Kent	7 gns.
5.	Sandwich, Kent	7 gns.
6.	Sandwich, Kent	10 gns.
7.	Spanish Beggar	35 gns.
8.	The Red House	25 gns.
9.	The Green House	15 gns.
10.	The Posada	30 gns.
11.	The White House	15 gns.
12.	Another Spanish Beggar	35 gns.
13.	Cordova	30 gns.
14.	A Mountain Town	15 gns.
15.	San Pancrazio, Taormina	17 gns.
16.	Ledda	12 gns.
17.	El Hadaddi	60 gns.
18.	Forum, Rome	10 gns.
19.	Via Appia	10 gns.
20.	The Stone Pine	15 gns.
21.	Forum, Rome	10 gns.
22.	Piazza del Popolo	10 gns.
23.	El Fondak	45 gns.
24.	Shopping in Tetuan	17 gns.
25.	Tangier	17 gns.
26.	La Rache	17 gns.
27.	Al Kassar	17 gns.
28.	Arzila	17 gns.
29.	Posada	20 gns.
30.	Trajan's Column	8 gns.
31.	Water Carrier	17 gns.
32.	Piazza Cappucini	15 gns.
33.	Spanish Village	20 gns.
34.	Early Spring	7 gns.

Canadian National Exhibition, Toronto

55.	Shopping in Morocco *oil*	$263
56.	The Blue Door, Tetuan *oil*	263

1915

Canadian Art Club, Toronto, Eighth Annual
Exhibition 7-30 October

"The Italian Set"   *lithotints*

110.   Lion of St. Mark, Venice
111.   Bridge, Venice
112.   Piazza Labia, Venice
113.   Piazza del Popolo, Rome
114.   Temple of Vesta, Rome
115.   Randazzo, Sicily
116.   Baptistry, Florence
117.   Piazza San Lorenzo, Florence
118.   Piazza San Firenze, Florence

"The Spanish Set"   *lithographs*

119.   The Grandmother
120.   The Oil Seller
121.   The Water Carrier
122.   The Old Horse
123.   Tetuan
124.   The Spanish Beggar

"English Subjects"   *lithographs*

125.   Boston
126.   Boston
127.   Stratford-on-Avon

Leicester Galleries, London   6th Senefelder Club
Exhibition   December

"The Spanish Gypsy" series

1919

Royal Academy of Arts, London
Canadian War Memorials Exhibtion

Ypres, The Footprint of the Hun

Anderson Galleries, New York
Canadian War Memorials Exhibition

36.   Ypres, The Cloth Hall

National Gallery of Canada, Ottawa
Canadian War Memorials Exhibition

The Cloth Hall, Ypres

1920

Selections from the war collection, including
Arras . . ., were shown at the National Gallery of
Canada and Canadian National Exhibition in 1920.

1922

Venice Biennale, British Section

54.   Portrait of a Warrior
55.   Abbozzo Moresco

1924

British Empire Exhibition, London, Palace of Arts
April-October

F15.   Adoration of the Shepherds
F38.   The Annunciation
BB41.   Major Anderson

1926

Beaux Arts Gallery, London

James Kerr-Lawson   January

[Copy of catalogue unlocated. Works listed are
mentioned in reviews.]

Paintings:

Pine Tree Near Pompeii
Assisi
Taormina
Snow on Monte Morello, Florence
Rimini
Church of Sta. Catalina, Palma
Farm on Romney Marsh

Paper mosaics:

The Annunciation
The Adoration of the Shepherds

Drawings:

William de Morgan
Lady Paget
Maurice Hewlett
F. Brangwyn
Self-portrait

Watercolour:

Cutting Withies, Kent

Lithotints:

Italian subjects

1930

Beaux Arts Gallery, London

Exhibition of Paintings of Spain and Morocco by
James Kerr-Lawson   20 October - 8 November

Paintings:

1.   Palma
2.   Portrait of Major A.
3.   Moorish Street Scene
4.   City Gates
5.   The Dream
6.   The Soko
7.   Lady of Granada
8.   Città di Castello
9.   Fonda
10.   Courtyard
11.   Leghorn
12.   Seamstresses

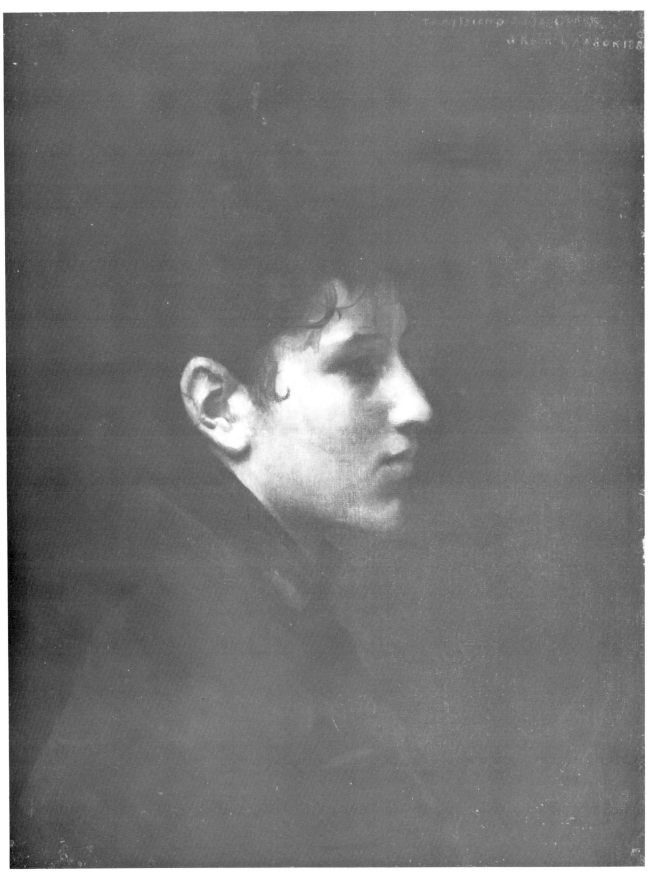

10 *Study of a Girl* 1888

13. Town Gate
14. Ajaccio
15. Ajaccio, the Port
16. On the Lagoons
17. Ravenna
18. Moorish Market Place
19. Tetuan
20. Moorish Scene, Tetuan

Watercolours:

21. Prato
22. Segovia
23. Arch of Titus
24. Boston
25. Clair de Lune, Assisi
26. Bridge at Rimini
27. Study of Devonshire Fishermen
28. Cathedral, Palma
29. Viterbo
30. Santillana
31. Rome

1942

Beaux Arts Gallery, London

James Kerr-Lawson Memorial Exhibition
November-December

[Copy of catalogue unlocated. About 50 works said to be included. Works listed are mentioned in reviews.]

Paintings:

Winter in Kent
Boston, Lincolnshire
E. V. Lucas
Verlaine
Marketplace, Tangier
White Arab Horse
John Logie Baird
Col. J. S. Anderson
F. Brangwyn in Moorish Dress

Watercolours:

Outside the Walls, Pompeii
Street in Rome
Ajaccio
Mantua
Segovia
Devon fishermen

Drawings:

H. G. Wells
A. S. Hartrick

1947

Hazlitt Gallery, London

Exhibition of Paintings and Watercolours by
J. Kerr-Lawson (1864-1939) 11-29 March

[Copy of catalogue unlocated. At least 80 works said to be included.]

1948

Beaux Arts Gallery, London

Exhibition of Drawings and Watercolours by
Some Eminent English XXth Century Artists
27 April - 14 May

32. Florence *wc*		20 gns.
33. Hammersmith *wc*		12 gns.
34. Boston, Lincolnshire *o/paper*		15 gns.
35. Palma, Majorca *o/paper*		12 gns.
36. Mantua *wc*		40 gns.
37. Siena *o/paper*		12 gns.
38. Assisi *wc*		15 gns.
39. Piazza, Siena *wc*		20 gns.
40. Città di Castello *wc*		12 gns.

The Heffer Gallery, Cambridge

Paintings and Drawings by the late
James Kerr-Lawson 27 April - 22 May

Paintings:

1. Portrait of Victor Hugo, 1883-84
2. A Landscape in Italy
3. In Cordova
4. "Lola"
5. "Diana"
6. "The Wayside Madonna", Segovia
7. In the Podere, Tuscany
8. A Spanish Peasant Family
9. On a Dutch Canal
10. Haymaking in Kent
11. The Generatiffe from the Alhambra
12. The Spinning Wheel
13. The Horses *(oil sketch on paper)*
14. "After the Heat of the Day"
15. A Street Scene in Spain
16. A Spanish Beggar
17. The Fruit Vendor
18. Homewards at Sunset
19. The Gipsy Water Carrier
20. Fisherboys playing among the Rocks
21. Behind the Village
22. "Jeannie"
23. A Sketch in Kent
24. Evening in Venice
25. The Windmill, Sandwich, 1910
26. Messina: Apse of Cathedral after Earthquake
27. Venice
28. Sandwich, 1910
29. "Inez"
30. A Sketch in Kent
31. The Farm Cart
32. The Cyprus Tree
33. A Street Scene in Spain
34. "Abdullah"
35. Mother and Child
36. The Statue
37. Boston Stump, Lincolnshire
38. "L'Equipage", Pas de Calais
39. In the Hague
40. Siena *(oil sketch on paper)*
41. A Woman Sewing
42. Butcher's Shop in Taormina
43. Landscape in Italy
44. In the Market

45. The Boat Builders
46. The Spinning Wheel
47. Segovia
48. L'Arrullo
49. A Moorish Market
50. "Billy"

Drawings:

51. Segovia
52. Colleone
53. A Canal Scene in Venice
54. Verona
55. Siena
56. In Corsica
57. Taormina
58. Mediterranean Fisherfolk
59. Near Florence
60. Fivizzano, in the Luni Giana
61. The Courtyard
62. Viareggio
63. The Grand Canal, Venice
64. Shop Door in Taormina
65. Venice
66. Siena
67. Outside the Walls, Pompeii
68. On the Thames
69. Palma, Marjorca
70. Siena
71. Portrait of A. S. Hartrick
72. "The Presentation"
73. Portrait of E. V. Lucas
74. In Majorca
75. The Grand Canal, Venice
76. "Poor Sue"
77. Portrait of F. Derwent Wood
78. The Tailor's Shop
79. Portrait of H. G. Wells
80. "The Toilet"

Ferens Art Gallery, Hull

Exhibition of Paintings by James Kerr-Lawson, 1864-1939   October

Oil Paintings:

1.	The Spinning Wheel	£30
2.	Peddlar and Geese	£40
3.	Evening in Venice	£40
4.	After the Heat of the Day	£40
5.	Boston, Lincs.	£40
6.	Italian Landscape	£30
7.	Street Scene in Spain	£35
8.	Mother and Child	£30
9.	A Moorish Market	£35
10.	Inez	£55
11.	Jeannie	£60
12.	The Farm Cart	£40
13.	L'Arullo	£50
14.	Homewards at Sunset	£40
15.	Lazarillo	£75
16.	The Wayside Madonna, Segovia	£40
17.	A Spanish Family	£25
18.	In Cordova	£25
19.	Billy	£20
20.	Abdulla	£30
21.	In the Podere, Tuscany	£35
22.	Gipsy Water Carrier	£25
23.	Fisherboys Playing among Rocks	£45
24.	Haymaking in Kent	£35

25.	The Generatiffe from the Alhambra	£25
26.	Woman Sewing	£25
27.	The Statue	£20
28.	Venice	£35
29.	Woman Spinning	£25
30.	On a Dutch Canal	£25
31.	A Spanish Beggar	£35
32.	Landscape in Italy	£25
33.	The Boat Builders	£30
34.	Segovia	£100
35.	Diana	£100
36.	Allegory of Fortune	£100
37.	Messina	£100
38.	Boston, Lincs.	£65
39.	A Sketch in Kent	£10
40.	Landscape Sketch	£10
41.	The Cypress Tree	£20
42.	Spanish Street Scene	£20
43.	Butcher's Shop, Taormina	£30
44.	Portrait of Joseph Pennell	£40
45.	L'Equipage, Pas de Calais	£20
46.	Fruit Vendor	£15
47.	Sir Frank Brangwyn, R.A.	
48.	Rubio	
49.	Sir John Lavery	
50.	Ruins at Taormina	£35
51.	Taormina	£40
52.	Village Scene with Fountain	£40
53.	Quayside with Fishermen	£30
54.	Palma, Marjorca	£25
55.	Harvesting	£15
56.	River Scene with Bridge	£25
57.	Beggar	£15
58.	Harvesting	£15
59.	Fisherman	£30
60.	Farmer with Scythe	£30
61.	Cottages	£20
62.	Harvesting	£15
63.	The Horses	£20

Drawings:

64.	Segovia	£75
65.	Colleone	£10
66.	Canal Scene, Venice	£15
67.	Mediterranean Fisherfolk	£25
68.	Siena	£20
69.	Taormina	£10
70.	Verona	£15
71.	H. G. Wells	£25
72.	E. V. Lucas	£25
73.	A. S. Hartrick	£25
74.	F. Derwent Wood	£25
75.	Harvesting	£15
76.	Harvesting, S. Giorgio	£12
77.	L'Obelisco	£12
78.	Harvesting	£12
79.	Shop Door in Taormina	£10
80.	On the Thames	£15
81.	The Presentation	£15
82.	The Toilet	£15
83.	Fivizzano, in the Luni Giana	£55

Beaux Arts Gallery, London

Exhibition of Paintings and Water Colours by James Kerr-Lawson   26 October - 19 November

1.	Florence	wc	25 gns.
2.	Hammersmith	wc	15 gns.

3.	Boston *o/paper*	16 gns.
4.	Mantua *wc*	40 gns.
5.	Siena *o/paper*	14 gns.
6.	Assisi *wc*	15 gns.
7.	Piazza Siena *wc*	26 gns.
8.	Città di Castello *wc*	12 gns.
9.	Near Pisa *wc*	14 gns.
10.	Boats at Livorno *wc*	15 gns.
11.	Front at Livorno *wc*	15 gns.
12.	Greek Theatre, Taormina *wc*	17 gns.
13.	Canal Scene, Holland *wash*	8 gns.
14.	Near Sandwich, Kent *wc*	10 gns.
15.	Street, Ile Rousse Corsica *wc*	12 gns.
16.	Segovia *wc*	14 gns.
17.	View, Sandwich, Kent *wc*	12 gns.
18.	View, Sandwich, Kent *wc*	14 gns.
19.	Fonda, Cordoba *o/paper*	14 gns.
20.	Outskirts, Palma *wc*	20 gns.
21.	On the Arno *o/paper*	14 gns.
22.	Street in Tuscany *o/paper*	12 gns.
23.	Tuscan Town *o/paper*	12 gns.
24.	Gubbio *o/paper*	17 gns.
25.	Church, Ile Rousse, Corsica *wc*	20 gns.
26.	Church of Carmine, Florence *wc*	22 gns.
27.	Temple of Vesta, Rome *wc*	22 gns.
28.	La fontana, Taormina *wc*	25 gns.
29.	Boats in Harbour, Ajaccio *wc*	20 gns.
30.	Palma di Majorca *wc*	15 gns.
31.	Bazaar, Tangier *o/paper*	15 gns.
32.	Mules, Morocco *wc*	12 gns.
33.	Near Città di Castello *wash*	10 gns.
34.	Tetuan *wc*	12 gns.
35.	Viareggio *o/paper*	15 gns.
36.	On Side of Vesuvius *wc*	14 gns.
37.	Lucca *o/paper*	14 gns.
38.	Palma *o/paper*	16 gns.
39.	Ajaccio *wc*	17 gns.
40.	Bay at Livorno *wc*	17 gns.
41.	Fishermen, Palma *wc*	30 gns.
42.	Grand Canal, Venice *wc*	30 gns.
43.	Siena, *drwg.*	20 gns.
44.	Outside Walls, Pompeii *wc*	20 gns.
45.	Peasants, Fonda, Cordoba *wc*	20 gns.
46.	View, Grand Canal, Venice *wc*	20 gns.
47.	Forum, Rome, Trajan's Column *oil*	150 gns.
48.	Arch of Constantine *oil*	150 gns.
49.	Greek Theatre, Taormina *wc*	35 gns.
50.	Palma, Majorca *oil*	100 gns.
51.	The Hague *oil*	45 gns.
52.	Patio, Grenada *oil*	35 gns.
53.	Corte, Corsica *wc*	30 gns.
54.	Mrs. Aubrey Waterfield *silverpoint*	35 gns.

1949

Messrs. T. & R. Annan and Sons Ltd., Glasgow

Exhibition of Works by James Kerr-Lawson,
1864-1939   February

1.	The Front at Livorno	15 gns.
2.	Evening on the Apennines	10 gns.
3.	Piazza, Siena	20 gns.
4.	Fonda, Cordoba	14 gns.
5.	Greek Theatre, Taormina	35 gns.
6.	In Hills, Umbria	10 gns.
7.	Fieldworker, Northbourne, Kent	10 gns.

8.	Poor Sue	25 gns.
9.	Serving Mass, Siena	12 gns.
10.	Siena Cathedral	14 gns.
11.	Street, Fivizzano	35 gns.
12.	In Holland	10 gns.
13.	Boats in Harbour, Ajaccio	20 gns.
14.	Chioggia	13 gns.
15.	Hammersmith	15 gns.
16.	Taormina	35 gns.
17.	Ferry on Arno, Florence	15 gns.
18.	Fishermen, Palma, Majorca	30 gns.
19.	Cambria	18 gns.
20.	Venice from S. Giorgio	35 gns.
21.	Tetuan	12 gns.
22.	Near Pisa	14 gns.
23.	Città di Castello, Umbria	10 gns.
24.	Mules, Morocco	12 gns.
25.	Gateway, Bergamo	35 gns.
26.	Shrine, Settignano	12 gns.
27.	Street, Tuscany	12 gns.
28.	Trajan's Column	150 gns.
29.	Learning to Read	35 gns.
30.	Ruins, Inexina	50 gns.
31.	Old Log House, Blair	35 gns.
32.	Arch of Constantine	150 gns.
33.	Going to Market, Morocco	12 gns.
34.	Outskirts, Palma	20 gns.
35.	Boats at Livorno	15 gns.
36.	At Fair near Florence	17 gns.
37.	Palma, Majorca	100 gns.
38.	Courtyard in Kent	25 gns.
39.	Madonna of Gypsies	12 gns.
40.	Church of Carmine, Florence	22 gns.
41.	Bay, Livorno	17 gns.
42.	Square, Taormina	25 gns.
43.	Ruins, Ypres	25 gns.
44.	Sta. Maria della Salute, Venice	100 gns.
45.	London Sketch	25 gns.
46.	Moroccan Street Scene	25 gns.
47.	Viareggio	15 gns.
48.	Siena	20 gns.
49.	Gipsy Water Carrier, Cordova	30 gns.
50.	Patio, Granada	35 gns.
51.	Church Interior, Palma	100 gns.
52.	Gubbio	17 gns.
53.	Fontana, Taormina	25 gns.
54.	Palma, Church with Tower	12 gns.
55.	Spanish Memories	10 gns.
56.	Grand Canal, Venice	30 gns.
57.	View, Grand Canal, Venice	20 gns.
58.	Street, Ile Rousse, Corsica	12 gns.
59.	Pistoia	20 gns.
60.	Assisi	15 gns.
61.	Temple of Vesta, Rome	22 gns.
62.	Canal Scene, Holland	8 gns.

1952

Institut Français d'Ecosse, Edinburgh

Exhibition of Works by J. Kerr-Lawson   March

1.	Umbrian Landscape *H. M. Queen Mary*
2.	Caterina *Mrs. Kerr-Lawson*
3.	Self-Portrait *Col. Waite and Hon. Mrs. Waite*
4.	Veiled Lady *Mrs. Kerr-Lawson*
5.	Lady Paget *Mr. and Mrs. Charles Williams*

7 The Artist's Mother in Wicker Chair [undated]

1983

Art Gallery of Windsor, Windsor, Ontario
James Kerr-Lawson: A Canadian Abroad

34 *London Bridge   ca. 1906-07*

BIBLIOGRAPHY

Archival Sources

Andover, Massachusetts. Mrs. Peter F. Groff. Lawson family archives.

Edinburgh. National Register Office of Scotland. Lawson family birth and marriage records.

Florence. Villa I Tatti. Bernard Berenson Archives.

Glasgow. University Library. Dugald Sutherland MacColl papers.

Hamilton, Ontario. Art Gallery of Hamilton. William Blair Bruce papers.

Hamilton, Ontario. Hamilton Public School Board. Archives.

London. The British Library. Maurice Hewlett diaries.

London. Chelsea Arts Club. Club records.

London. Chelsea Library. James Kerr-Lawson clippings file.

London. Imperial War Museum. War artists files.

London. National Register Office of England. Kerr-Lawson marriage and death records.

London. Royal Academy Library. Sir George Clausen diaries.

London. Victoria and Albert Museum, National Art Library. Exhibition catalogue files.

London. Witt Library. Kerr-Lawson photographic file.

Montreal. McCord Museum. William Brymner papers.

Montreal. Museum of Fine Arts Library. Kerr-Lawson clippings file.

New York. The Frick Reference Library. Photographic files.

Ottawa. National Gallery of Canada. Robert Harris papers.

Ottawa. National Gallery of Canada. Homer Watson papers.

Ottawa. National Gallery of Canada Library. Kerr-Lawson clippings file.

Toronto. Art Gallery of Ontario Library. Kerr-Lawson clippings file.

Toronto. Metropolitan Central Library. Kerr-Lawson clippings file.

Toronto. Ontario Provincial Archives. Ontario Society of Artists, Minute and Letter books.

Champaign-Urbana. University of Illinois Library. H. G. Wells Collection.

Washington, D. C. Library of Congress. Joseph and Elizabeth Pennell papers.

Writings by James Kerr-Lawson

"Carlo Coppoli." *Apollo,* January 1934, p. 54, repr.

"Frank Brangwyn's Inexhaustible Genius." *Saturday Night,* 28 June 1924, p. 3.

"The Influence of the Franciscan Legend on Italian Art." In *Assisi of St. Francis,* by Mrs. Robert Goff. Chatto and Windus: London, 1908.

"A Newly 'Discovered' Portrait of Verlaine." *Apollo,* May 1939, pp. 262-63, repr.

"Points from Letters—A Chinese Superstition." *The Times,* (London), 28 June 1927.

"Portrait of Lorenzo Lotto By Himself." *The Burlington Magazine,* March 1905, pp. 453-54.

"Tempera: A New Light on an Old Method." *The Magazine of Art,* September 1903, pp. 560-63, repr.

"Two Portraits of William Blundell Spence." *The Burlington Magazine,* June 1904, pp. 310-19.

Books

Adams, John Coldwell. *Seated with the Mighty: A biography of Sir Gilbert Parker.* Ottawa: Borealis Press, 1979.

Arts and Letters Club of Toronto. *The Year Book of Canadian Art 1913.* London: J. M. Dent & Sons, 1913.

Beaverbrook Art Gallery Paintings. Fredericton: University Press of New Brunswick, 1959.

Belleroche, William de. *Brangwyn's Pilgrimage.* London: Chapman and Hall, 1948.

Berger, Carl. *The Sense of Power: Studies in the Ideas of Canadian Imperialism 1867-1914.*
    Toronto: University of Toronto Press, 1970.

Blunt, Reginald. *An illustrated Historical Handbook to the Parish of Chelsea.* London: Lamley and Co., 1900.

Braide, Janet G. *William Brymner 1855-1925: A Retrospective.* Kingston: Agnes Etherington Art Centre, 1979.

Brangwyn, Rodney. *Brangwyn.* London: William Kimber, 1978.

Bury, Adrian. *Two Centuries of British Water-Colour Painting.* London: George Newnes Ltd., 1950.

The Canadian Art Club 1907-1911. Toronto, 1911.

Caw, James L. *Scottish Painting: Past and Present 1620-1908.* Bath: Kingsmead Reprints, 1975.

Chamot, Mary; Farr, Dennis; and Butlin, Martin. *The Tate Gallery: The Modern British paintings, drawings and sculptures.*
    2 vols. London: Oldbourne Press, 1964.

Dodgson, Campbell, and Pennell, Joseph. *The Senefelder Club.* London: Twenty-One Gallery, 1922.

Farr, Dennis. *English Art 1870-1940.* Oxford History of English Art, vol. 11. Oxford: Clarendon Press, 1978.

Fry, Roger. *The Letters.* Edited by Denys Sutton. London: Chatto and Windus, 1972.

Godenrath, Percy Francis. *Lest We Forget: The Story of the Canadian War Memorials Collection of Art.*
    Ottawa: King's Printer, 1934.

Goff, Mrs. Robert. *Assisi of St. Francis.* London: Chatto and Windus, 1908

Goodison, J. W. *Fitzwilliam Museum Cambridge, Catalogue of Paintings. Vol. III: The British School.*
    Cambridge: Cambridge University Press, 1977.

Harper, J. Russell. *Painting in Canada: A History.* 2nd ed. Toronto: University of Toronto Press, 1977.

Hartrick, A. S. *A Painter's Pilgrimage Through Fifty Years.* Cambridge: At the University Press, 1939.

Hewlett, Maurice. *Earthwork Out of Tuscany.* London: J. M. Dent and Co., 1900.

_____.*The Road in Tuscany.* 2 vols. London: Macmillan and Co., 1904.

_____.*The Letters.* Edited by Laurence Binyon. London: Methuen and Co. Ltd., 1926.

Hubbard, Robert H. *The National Gallery of Canada, Catalogue of Paintings and Sculpture. Vol. II:*
    Modern European Schools. Toronto: University of Toronto Press, 1959.

_____.*Some artists who have lived and worked in Hamilton.* Hamilton: Art Gallery of Hamilton, 1967.

Hutton, Edward. *Country Walks about Florence.* London: Methuen and Co. Ltd., 1908.

Illustrated Souvenir of the Palace of Arts: British Empire Exhibition (1924). London: Fleetway Press Ltd., 1924.

Jackson, Alexander Young. *A Painter's Country.* Toronto: Clarke Irwin, 1958.

Johnson, J. and Greutzner, A. *The Dictionary of British Artists 1880-1940.* Woodbridge, Suffolk:
    Antique Collectors' Club, 1976.

Kallmann, Helmut. *A History of Music in Canada.* Toronto: University of Toronto Press, 1960.

Kerr-Lawson, Edward. *A Catalogue of Paintings in the Prado, Madrid.* London: William Heinemann, 1896.

Lavery, John. *The Life of a Painter.* London: Cassell and Company Ltd., 1940.

Massé, H. J. L. J. *The Art Workers Guild 1884-1934.* Oxford: Art Workers Guild, 1935.

McConkey, Kenneth. *Sir George Clausen R.A. 1852-1944.* Bradford: Bradford Art Galleries and Museums, 1980.

Miller, Muriel. *Homer Watson.* Toronto: Ryerson Press, 1938.

Nasby, Judith M. *The University of Guelph Art Collection.* Guelph: University of Guelph, 1980.

100 Years: Evolution of the Ontario College of Art. Toronto: Art Gallery of Ontario, 1977.

Page, Frank E. *Homer Watson: Artist and Man.* Kitchener: Commerical Printing Co., 1939.

Pennell, Elizabeth Robins and Joseph. *The Life of James McNeill Whistler.* London: William Heinemann, 1908.

_____.*The Whistler Journal.* Philadelphia: J. B. Lippincott Co., 1921.

Pennell, Elizabeth Robins. *The Life and Letters of Joseph Pennell.* Boston: Little, Brown and Co., 1929.

Pennell, Joseph. *Cantor Lecture on Artistic Lithography,* London: Royal Society of Arts, 1914.

_____.*Lithographers and Lithography.* London: T. Fisher Unwin, 1915.

Reid, Dennis. *A Concise History of Canadian Painting.* Toronto: Oxford University Press, 1973.

Ross, Janet. *The Fourth Generation.* London: Constable and Co. Ltd., 1912.

Rothenstein, William. *Men and Memories.* 2 vols. London: Faber and Faber, 1931-32.

Royal Academy of Arts. *An Exhibition of Original Posters Designed for the Empire Marketing Board.* London, 1926.

Salaman, Malcolm C. *Modern Woodcuts and Lithographs by British and French Artists.* London: The Studio Ltd., 1919.

Samuels, Ernest. *Bernard Berenson: The Making of a Connoisseur.* Cambridge: Belknap Press of Harvard University Press, 1979.

Skipwith, Peyton. *The Rustic Image: Rural Themes in British Painting 1880-1912.* London: The Fine Art Society Ltd., 1979.

Sparrow, Walter Shaw. *Advertising and British Art.* London: John Lane, 1924.

Strickland-Constable, Miranda, and Robertson, Alexander. *Concise Catalogue: Leeds City Art Galleries.* Leeds: Leeds City Council, 1976.

Thomson, Duncan, and Lockhart, Sheila Bruce. *Scottish National Portrait Gallery: Concise Catalogue.* Edinburgh: Trustees of the National Galleries of Scotland, 1977.

Gli Uffizi: Catalogo Generale. Florence: Centro Di, 1979.

Van Every, Jane. *With Faith, Ignorance and Delight: Homer Watson.* Doon: Homer Watson Trust, 1967.

Vaughan, Francis E. *Andrew C. Lawson: Scientist, Teacher, Philosopher.* Glendale, California: The Arthur H. Clark Company, 1970.

Walker Art Gallery. *Merseyside Painters, People and Places: Catalogue of Oil Paintings.* 2 vols. Liverpool: Merseyside County Council, 1978.

Waterfield, Lina. *Castle in Italy: An Autobiography.* London: John Murray, 1961.

Watts, Mary S. *George Frederick Watts.* 3 vols. London: Macmillan and Co. Ltd., 1912.

Whyte, Frederic. *William Heinemann: A Memoir.* Garden City, N.Y.: Doubleday Doran and Co. Inc., 1929.

Weisberg, Gabriel P. *The Realist Tradition: French Painting and Drawing 1830-1900.* Cleveland: Cleveland Museum of Art, 1980.

Yung, K. K. *National Portrait Gallery: Complete Illustrated Catalogue 1856-1979.* New York: St. Martin's Press, 1981.

Articles (in chronological order)

1883

"The Art Gallery." *The Witness* (Montreal), 11 April 1883.

"The Art Exhibition." *The Gazette* (Montreal), 16 April 1883.

"The Art Exhibition." *The Globe* (Toronto), 26 May 1883.

1884

"Deaths: David Allan Smith." *Hamilton Spectator,* 1 May 1884.

"In Memoriam: David Smith." *Hamilton Spectator,* 10 May 1884.

1885

"The Spring Exhibition." *The Gazette* (Montreal), 28 April 1885.

1886

"Royal Academy Exhibition." *The Citizen* (Ottawa), 3 February 1886.

"Original Drawings." *The Herald* (Montreal), October 1886.

1887

"Art: Mr. Lawson's New Picture." *The Week* (Toronto), 17 March 1887, p. 257.

"Art: Mr. Lawson's New Picture." *Hamilton Spectator,* 17 March 1887.

"Rembrandt House." *The Week* (Toronto), 20 October 1887, p. 760.

"Art and Artists." *Toronto Saturday Night,* 10 December 1887, p. 10.

1888

"Among Canadian Artists." *The Gazette* (Montreal), 7 April 1888.

1889

Nemo [pseud.] "Art and Artists." *Toronto Saturday Night,* 16 March 1889, p. 7.

Van [pseud.] "Art and Artists." *Toronto Saturday Night,* 1 June 1889, p. 7.

1893

"The Chronicle of Art: Exhibitions." *The Magazine of Art,* April 1893, p. xxvii.

1898

Sauter, George. "The International Society of Painters, Sculptors and Gravers," *The Studio,* August 1898, p. 110.

1899

Grant, Jean. "Studio and Gallery." *Saturday Night,* 30 December 1899, p. 9.

1903

"Messrs. Dowdeswell's Gallery." *The Athenaeum,* 11 April 1903, p. 473.

"Minor Art Exhibitions." *The Times* (London), 14 April 1903.

"London Exhibitions." *The Magazine of Art,* June 1903, pp. 422-23, repr.

1906

"Exhibitions." *The Times* (London), 11 June 1906.

1908

"St. Paul's Cathedral, London." *The Neolith* I (1908): repr. opp. p. 24.

"Canadian Art is Given Fresh Stimulus." *Toronto World,* 4 February 1908.

1909

"Art: The International Society." *The Times* (London), 9 January 1909.

"The International Society's Ninth Exhibition." *International Studio* (London), April 1909, p. 132.

1912

Welch, Charles. "Henry Hucks Gibbs, 1st Baron Aldenham." *Dictionary of National Biography,* Second Supplement, s.v.

"Canadian Art Club's Fifth Exhibition." *The News* (Toronto), 12 February 1912.

"Mr. Edward Kerr-Lawson: found shot." *The Times* (London), early edition, 20 September 1912, p. 4.

"Studio Talk: London." *The Studio,* October 1912, pp. 312-16, repr.

1913

Borenius, Tancred. "An Unpublished Portrait by Moroni in the Collection of James Kerr-Lawson." *The Burlington Magazine,* March 1913, pp. 344-49.

"Fine Pictures at the Canadian Art Club Show." *The Globe* (Toronto), 10 May 1913.

1914

Pennell, Joseph. "The Senefelder Club and the Revival of Artistic Lithography." *The Studio,* February 1914, pp. 3-6, repr.

"Some Notable Etchings." *The Times* (London), 20 April 1914.

Charlesworth, Hector. "The Pictures of James Kerr-Lawson." *Saturday Night,* (Toronto), 20 June 1914, p. 4, repr.

_____. "Praise for a Canadian Painter." *Saturday Night,* 3 October 1914, p. 3

Loga, Valerian von. [Article on El Greco portrait in Kerr-Lawson collection.] *Jahrbuch der Koniglich Preussischen Kunstsammlungen,* 1914, pp. 43-51.

1916

"Current Art Notes: The Senefelder Club." *The Connoissseur,* January 1916, p. 55.

Charlesworth, Hector. "Studio Talk: Toronto." *The Studio,* May 1916, p. 274.

"What I Gave I Have." *Saturday Night,* 5 August 1916, p. 11, repr.

1917

"Deaths: Jessie Kerr-Lawson." *The Globe* (Toronto), 1 August 1917.

1918

"St. Paul's Cathedral, London." *The Canadian Magazine,* October 1918, p. 489, repr.

1919

"A Famous Canadian Painter at Work." *Saturday Night,* 20 September 1919, p. 7, repr.

Lismer, Arthur. "The Canadian War Memorials." *The Rebel,* October 1919, pp. 40-42.

1920

Charlesworth, Hector. "Reflections." *Saturday Night,* 18 September 1920, p. 2.

1921

"Arras Cathedral." *The Canadian Magazine,* June 1921, p. 145, repr.

"A Moorish Market." *Colour,* December 1921, p. 98, repr.

1922

"Portrait of Paul Verlaine," *Colour,* February 1922, p. 13, repr.

"The Warrior by James Kerr-Lawson." *Saturday Night,* 2 September 1922, p. 10, repr.

"Professor A. A. Lawson." *Saturday Night,* 9 September 1922, repr.

"El Haddadi (The Blacksmith's Shop)." *Colour,* November 1922, p. 78, repr.

"Winter in Kent." *Colour,* December 1922-January 1923, p. 100, repr.

1924

"Aldenham House, Hertfordshire." *Country Life,* 23 February 1924, pp. 282-90, repr.

Venturi, Adolfo. "Ritratto del Tintoretto Presso Kerr-Lawson a Londra." *L'Arte,* March-June 1924, pp. 77-78, repr.

"A Portrait by Tintoretto." *Saturday Night,* 11 October 1924, p. 5.

1925

"Wills and Bequests: Mrs. Eliza Muir Smith." *The Times* (London), 2 October 1925.

1926

"Art Exhibitions: Mr. Kerr-Lawson." *The Times* (London), 26 January 1926.

"Italy as Seen by a Scottish Artist of European Repute." *The Illustrated London News,* 13 February 1926, p. 261, repr.

"Art Notes." *Colour,* March 1926, p. 25.

Charlesworth, Hector. "The Kerr-Lawson Show in London." *Saturday Night,* 27 March 1926, p. 3.

"Joseph Pennell." *Saturday Night,* 1 May 1926, p. 3, repr.

"Self-Portrait of James Kerr-Lawson and Prof. Andrew Cowper Lawson, LL.D." *Saturday Night,* 8 May 1926, p. 3.

Hartrick, A. S. "James Kerr-Lawson's Decorative Panels." *Saturday Night,* 19 June 1926, p. 5, repr.

" 'Assisi' " by James Kerr-Lawson." *The Times* (London), 28 June 1926, repr.

Charlesworth, Hector. "Famous Artist." *Saturday Night,* 30 July 1926.

" 'The Annunciation' Decorative Panel by J. Kerr-Lawson." *The Studio,* October 1926, pp. 275, 278-79, repr.

1927

Dodgson, Campbell. "James Kerr-Lawson." in Ulrich Thieme and Felix Becker, *Allgemeines Lexikon der Bildenden Kunstler,* s.v.

Lessore, Frederick. "The Decorative Paintings of James Kerr-Lawson." *The Studio,* January 1927, pp. 26-28, repr.

Furst, Herbert. " 'The Adoration of the Shepherds': A Paper Mosaic by J. Kerr-Lawson." *Apollo,* October 1927, pp. 183-85, repr.

"Two Famous British Painters." *Saturday Night,* 12 November 1927, p. 1, repr.

1929

Charlesworth, Hector. "Kerr-Lawson and the Moors." *Saturday Night,* 20 July 1929, p. 3.

1930

"Portrait of Andrew C. Lawson," *Saturday Night,* 12 April 1930, p. 13, repr.

"Exhibitions: James Kerr-Lawson." *The Times* (London), 22 October 1930.

"Books of the Day." *The Illustrated London News,* 25 October 1930, p. 716, repr.

Parks, Kineton. "Kerr-Lawson at the Beaux Arts Gallery." *Apollo,* November 1930, pp. 367-68, repr.

"The Dream," *Saturday Night,* 13 December 1930, p. 1, repr.

1931

Charlesworth, Hector. "The Turn of the Wheel: James Kerr-Lawson." *Canadian Home Journal,*
    February 1931, pp. 18, 55, repr.

"Portrait of Mrs. W. H. Cawthra." *Saturday Night,* 22 August 1931, p. 11, repr.

"Bust of Charles James Fox to Canadian Archives." *The Times* (London), 12 June 1931, repr.

Ruthenburg, Grace D. "J. B. Speed Museum Notes." *Louisville Courier Journal* (Kentucky), 18 October 1931.

"Speed Museum Panel Display Attracts Many." *Louisville Herald Post* (Kentucky), 19 October 1931.

1934

"Drawing of E. V. Lucas." *Saturday Night,* 28 April 1934, p. 10, repr.

"A Famous Royal Academician as a Moorish Chief: Mr. Frank Brangwyn." *The Illustrated London News,*
    10 October 1934, repr.

1936

"Donor of His Works to Bruges and Honoured as Her 'Glorious Son'." The Illustrated London News,
    8 August 1936, p. 247, repr.

"Portrait of Frank Brangwyn." *The Times* (London), 14 August 1936, repr.

"Portrait of Frank Brangwyn." *Apollo,* September 1936, p. 176, repr.

"International Art News: London." *The Studio,* November 1936, p. 286, repr.

1938

"Portrait of A. S. Hartrick." *The Times* (London), 28 June 1938, repr.

"Portrait of E. V. Lucas." *The Studio,* October 1938, p. 218, repr.

1939

"Mr. James Kerr-Lawson: Mural Decoration and Portraits." *The Times* (London), 3 May 1939.

"Noted Artist Dies; Once Resided Here." *Hamilton Spectator,* 3 May 1939.

"Letter of Tribute." *The Times* (London), 4 May 1939.

"Noted Artist Dies in London." *The Globe and Mail* (Toronto), 4 May 1939, repr.

"Funerals: James Kerr-Lawson." *The Times* (London), 5 May 1939.

"Noted Scottish Artist: The Late Mr. James Kerr-Lawson." *Glasgow Herald,* 5 May 1939.

"Tribute from C. H. Turnor." *The Times* (London), 6 May 1939.

"Mr. J. Kerr-Lawson, Queen Mary's Message of Sympathy." *The Scotsman* (Edinburgh), 8 May 1939.

"Mr. J. Kerr-Lawson: Funeral of Famous Artist." *West London Press,* 12 May 1939.

"The Late James Kerr-Lawson." *Apollo,* June 1939, p. 311, repr.

Brangwyn, Frank. "Obituary. J. Kerr-Lawson: An Appreciation." *The Studio,* June 1939, p. 33, repr.

1940

"Widow to get Pension." *The Times* (London), 26 April 1940.

1942

"Gift to Chelsea Library." *West London Press,* 18 September 1942.

"London News and Comment: Kerr-Lawson Pictures." *The Scotsman* (Edinburgh), 5 November 1942.

"Art Exhibitions." *The Times* (London), 11 November 1942.

"Exhibitions: Beaux Arts Gallery." *West London Press,* 13 November 1942.

Earp, T. W. "Artist Who Did Not Exhibit: Posthumous Show." *The Daily Telegraph* (London), 17 November 1942.

1943

"Verlaine Portrait: Publisher's Inspiration." *The Daily Telegraph* (London), 11 February 1943.

"Verlaine Portrait to Fitzwilliam Museum." *The Times* (London), 13 February 1943.

[Report of gift of Kerr-Lawson works to the National Gallery.] *The Gazette* (Montreal), 1 September 1943.

1947

"Picture from the Past." *The Evening Standard* (London), 17 March 1947.

McCullough, Charles R. "Art in Hamilton: James Kerr-Lawson." *Hamilton Spectator*, 22 March 1947.

Bury, Adrian. "James Kerr-Lawson, Painter (1864-1939)." *The Connoisseur*, June 1947, p. 131.

1949

Orwin, C. S. "Christopher Hatton Turnor." in *Dictionary of National Biography 1931-1940*, s.v.

"Scottish Painter of Picturesque." *Glasgow Herald*, 22 February 1949.

1952

"Kerr-Lawson's Paintings." *The Times* (London), 5 March 1952.

"James Kerr-Lawson." *The Connoisseur*, June 1952, p. 115, repr.

"Death Notices: Kerr-Lawson." *The Times* (London), 12 June 1952.

"Her Chelsea Salon." *The Daily Telegraph* (London), 20 June 1952.

1956

Vollmer, Hans. *Allgemeines Lexikon der Bildenden Kunstler des XX Jahrhunderts*. s.v. "James Kerr-Lawson."

1970

Page, Robert J. D. "Carl Berger and the intellectual origins of Canadian imperialist thought, 1867-1914." *Journal of Canadian Studies*, vol. 5, no. 3, pp. 39-49.

1971

Cole, Douglas. "The Problem of 'Nationalism' and 'Imperialism' in British Settlement Colonies." *Journal of British Studies*, May 1971, pp. 160-82.

1975

Wilkin, Karen. "On the Cover: James Kerr-Lawson's 'The Miner'." *Edmonton Art Gallery Bulletin*, July-August 1975, repr.

Cook, Terry. "George R. Parkin and the concept of Britannic Idealism." *Journal of Canadian Studies*, vol. 10, no. 3, pp. 15-31

1978

McConkey, Kenneth. "The Bouguereau of the Naturalists; Bastien-Lepage and British Art." Art History, I (1978): 371-82.

Christie, Manson and Woods Ltd. *Fine Victorian Pictures*. 21 July 1978, lots 64-74, repr.

Sotheby's Belgravia. *Victorian Paintings, Drawings and Watercolours*. 25 July, 1978, lot 288, repr.

Christie, Manson and Woods Ltd. *Fine Victorian Pictures*. 13 October 1978, lots 92-103, repr.

Sotheby's Belgravia. *Victorian Paintings, Drawings and Watercolours*. 28 November 1978, lot 173, repr.

1979

"Poor Sue." *The Burlington Magazine*, November 1979, p. 739, repr. no. 82.

8   Learning to Read   [undated]

JAMES KERR-LAWSON:

UN CANADIEN À L'ÉTRANGER

James Kerr-Lawson est un peintre canadien peu connu qui eut autrefois la faveur du public et qui la mérite d'ailleurs encore. Ses meilleures oeuvres sont remarquables par la beauté de leur composition, la pureté de leurs couleurs, le raffinement de leur technique et, souvent, par l'habileté de leur conception. D'abord réaliste, il fut fortement influencé par l'art de la Renaissance et il se tourna par la suite vers la peinture décorative. D'un point de vue formal ou philosophique, il n'a pas l'envergure d'un James Wilson Morrice ou d'un Ozias Leduc. Toutefois, son oeuvre se compare avantageusement à celle de ses contemporains canadiens: Horatio Walker, George Reid, Homer Watson, William Brymner ou Paul Peel.

D'un point de vue historique, Kerr-Lawson est particulièrement intéressant. Il ne fut ni un maître influent, ni un propagandiste ou un créateur d'institutions culturelles, mais plutôt un expatrié, qui poursuivait sa propre Muse dans un contexte international. Il avait également une réputation à l'échelle internationale et il comptait parmi ses relations des gens importants et innovateurs à cette époque. Au Canada, il connaissait tout aussi bien Homer Watson que William Brymner et il était membre du Canadian Art Club. À l'étranger, il était un familier de personnalités telles que George Frederick Watts, James McNeill Whistler ou Bernard Berenson, de groupes comme la Glasgow School et l'International Society et de mouvements comme ceux du renouveau en peinture murale ou en lithographie. Parmi ses contemporains canadiens, seuls Morrice et Walker entretinrent probablement des relations plus importantes et jouirent d'une plus grande réputation internationale. En 1908, Kerr-Lawson était considéré comme l'un des peintures canadiens qui occupaient

> une position respectée et éminente parmi les grands peintures du monde... [qui] ont fait honneur à leur pays d'origine tout en accédant personnellement à la notoriété.[1]

Toutefois, la réputation de Kerr-Lawson, et les relations qu'il s'était faites, n'étaient pas de celles que l'histoire a privilégiées. D'une part, il s'était expatrié au moins à quatre reprises et, s'il était apprécié dans plusieurs pays, c'était d'un petit nombre de personnes. On ne le connaît donc que très peu et il ne s'est pas attiré d'office l'intérêt des nationalistes. D'autre part, ses relations étaient britan-

niques et l'on accorde aujourd'hui plus de prestige à des influences françaises. Cependant, pour les artistes de la génération de Kerr-Lawson, le fait de s'expatrier, d'avoir une tendance cosmopolite et d'entretenir des relations avec la Grande-Bretagne, semblait un atout majeur.

Durant la seconde moitié du dix-neuvième siècle, la puissance et l'influence de la Grande-Bretagne au Canada étaient à leur zénith. La France pouvait prédominer en peinture mais la Grande-Bretagne avait une influence culturelle plus vaste et plus profonde. Les anglophones de la classe moyenne et de la haute société étaient fiers de la puissance britannique et du fait que le Canada était le pays le plus progressiste de l'empire, un empire qui pouvait leur permettre de réaliser pleinement les plus hautes ambitions humaines. L'importance de cette tradition impérialiste a été démontrée par des historiens comme Carl Berger.[2] Même les artistes qui n'avaient pas vraiment de préoccupations politiques, en connurent l'influence de plusieurs façons. Des peintres britanniques comme John Fraser, Lucius O'Brien et Frederic Marlett Bell-Smith ont été le pivot des sociétés d'artistes canadiens et ils ont naturellement professé ici leurs opinions pro-britanniques. C'était de Grande-Bretagne que venaient les musiciens les plus influents du Canada de même que les écrivains et les intellectuels les plus actifs. De plus, certains Canadiens allèrent compléter leur formation en Grande-Bretagne et y demeurèrent quelquefois pour poursuivre leur carrière. Des peintres comme Kerr-Lawson, Mary Bell Eastlake et Elizabeth A. Forbes élurent domicile en Grande-Bretagne. Ce fut également le cas pour des écrivains comme Sir Gilbert Parker, Lily Dougall et Grant Allen. Steven Leacock, qui demeura au Canada, était certainement un anglophile et un impérialiste enthousiaste. Plusieurs musiciens canadiens, tels qu'Emma Albani, Louise Edvina, Harry Field et Nora Clench, établirent leur résidence principale à Londres. Bien que l'influence britannique ait déjà perdu de son importance après la Première Guerre mondiale, elle servit tout de même de solide point de référence aux peintres du Groupe des Sept et à des écrivains comme Hugh McLennan. Des musiciens britanniques comme Healy Willan et Sir Ernest MacMillan, ont dominé la musique canadienne jusque dans les années cinquante. De plus,

---

1. D. R. Wilkie, président du Canadian Art Club, dans le *Toronto World,* 4 février 1908.

2. Carl Berger, *The Sense of Power,* University of Toronto Press: Toronto, 1970. Voir aussi les articles de la bibliographie dressée par Douglas Cole, Terry Cook et Robert J. D. Page.

grâce à des hommes comme Lord Beaverbrook et Vincent Massey, on conserva encore longtemps des liens commerciaux et politiques avec la Grande-Bretagne.

Kerr-Lawson est un peintre important dans le contexte de cette tradition britannique. Certaines de ses oeuvres sont excellentes et il présente beaucoup d'intérêt au point de vue historique. Il est à espérer qu'on lui accordera maintenant la considération qu'il mérite.

James Kerr-Lawson est né le 28 octobre 1862 à Cellardyke (qui fait maintenant partie d'Anstruther), un ancien port de pêche pour crevettiers, sur la côte sud du Fifeshire, en Écosse. Il était le second enfant de William Lawson et Jessie Kerr. William Lawson (1830-1913) était un matelot charpentier et un constructeur de bateaux issu d'une vieille famille de marins du Fifeshire. Jessie Kerr (1838-1917) était de naissance plus obscure. Bien que l'on ne soit pas certain de ses origines, on sait qu'elle a été élevée par un couple dont le nom de famille était Kerr, dans le village de St. Monance, près d'Anstruther. Ils parvinrent à lui faire suivre un cours d'institutrice à Édimbourg et, le 30 mai 1860, elle épousa William Lawson à l'Eglise d'Écosse de St. Monance. Quatorze mois plus tard naquit leur premier fils, Andrew Cowper. Il fut suivi, quinze mois plus tard, de James Kerr et, éventuellement, de trois autres garçons et de cinq filles.[3] En 1865, à la suite d'un naufrage qui l'avait laissé exposé aux intempéries, William Lawson commença à souffrir de troubles cardiaques et auditifs qui allaient, en huit ans, le rendre invalide; c'est donc à Jessie que revint la responsabilité de subvenir aux besoins de la famille. En 1866, elle le persuada d'émigrer au Canada et il s'établit à Hamilton, Ontario, où, pendant plusieurs années, il travailla comme menuisier dans un chantier naval. En 1869, le nom de la famille apparaît dans les annuaires à l'adresse 247 James Street North. Jessie contribuait déjà au revenu familial en tenant un petit magasin de nouveautés et d'articles de modes. Elle allait plus tard employer ses talents littéraires en devenant journaliste, puis collaboratrice attitrée de plusieurs journaux; elle écrivit également quatre romans et des recueils de poésie et devint une personnalité éminente dans son domaine. Encore aujourd'hui, son nom apparaît dans les dictionnaires de biographies canadiennes.[4] C'était une mère aimante mais aussi une ardente perfectionniste, qui transmit à ses enfants sa passion pour l'étude.

Kerr-Lawson et ses frères et soeurs fréquentèrent l'école élémentaire publique de Hamilton, puis le Colle-giate Institute où James fit ses humanités sous la direction de George Dickson, plus tard principal de l'Upper Canada College. Aussi doué que son frère Andrew, James manifestait déjà un talent artistique très prometteur. Dickson encouragea les ambitions des deux frères, et lorsque les études de James furent compromises par l'état précaire des finances familiales, ce fut Dickson qui lui vint en aide. Ceci se passait en 1879 alors que Kerr-Lawson entrait à la toute nouvelle Ontario School of Art de Toronto. Il y étudia sous la direction du peintre paysagiste Thomas Mower Martin et il se peut qu'il y ait subi l'influence de Robert Harris, jeune peintre réaliste qui venait d'arriver de Paris. Comme on n'a pas retrouvé ses travaux d'étudiant, on ne possède pas de preuves de l'influence éventuelle de Harris sur Kerr-Lawson; mais les premiers ouvrages connus de Kerr-Lawson, exécutés plusieurs années plus tard, présentent, comme ceux de Harris, beaucoup de simplicité, un grand souci de la luminosité et de l'équilibre dans la composition, des tonalités sombres et un coup de pinceau dégagé et généreux.

En avril 1880, Kerr-Lawson se vit décerner par son école le premier prix en dessin de base à main levée[5] et il décida d'aller parfaire ses études en Europe. Comme il avait un net penchant pour le classicisme, il se dirigea d'abord vers Rome, où il étudia brièvement à l'Académie de France à la Villa Medici et à l'Accademia di Belle Arte. Il en apprit davantage à fréquenter les lieux de rencontre des artistes, comme le Caffè Greco sur la Via Condotti. C'est là qu'il fit la connaissance de celui qui fut vraiment son premier maître, le peintre Luigi Galli (1820-1900). On ne sait pas exactement en quoi Galli a pu l'influencer, mais ce n'est probablement pas tant par le biais de ses propres peintures aux sujets symboliques et à la facture audacieuse, que par son enthousiasme pour l'art vénitien et pour les oeuvres de George Frederick Watts. En effet, la peinture de Watts et l'art des Vénitiens allaient plus tard jouer un rôle important dans la vie de Kerr-Lawson.

Il ne resta pas longtemps à Rome mais se rendit à Naples et à Capri, au sud de l'Italie, et il ne tarda pas à envoyer au pays des peintures qui devaient figurer aux expositions de 1882 et de 1883 de l'Académie royale des arts du Canada et de l'Association des beaux-arts de Montréal. On a maintenant perdu la trace de ces peintures mais les comptes rendus des journaux en ont fait mention. Le critique du *Witness* écrivait:

> M. Lawson, un autre peintre canadien accompli, expose trois pièces très ambitieuses et poétiques représentant le sud de l'Italie. Elles ont un certain côté inachevé qui laisse beaucoup de latitude à l'imagination. La charmille aux cactus est de

---

3. Les enfants de William et Jessie Lawson furent Andrew Cowper, James Kerr, Katharine Leslie, Elizabeth McKenzie, Alice-Margaret, William Leslie, Anstruther Abercrombie, Edward Kerr, Jessie Kerr et Jean.

4. *Macmillan Dictionary of Canadian Biography*, 4e édition, 1978, p. 449.

5. Ontario Society of Artists, registre des procès-verbaux, 22 avril 1880.

conception très heureuse et le paysage au crépuscule qui représente un chèvre se promenant à flanc de colline, évoque vraiment Capri, l'île des chèvres, site qui, paraît-il, a servi de modèle.[6]

Le critique du *Globe* décrivait ainsi *The Cactus Bower, Capri:*

> une scène tropicale où la gamme des couleurs représente avec justesse les flots de lumière solaire. On aperçoit un coin de ciel d'un bleu intense et l'on ne peut qu'admirer la façon dont il a su exécuter les taches sombres de l'ombre qui se mêlent aux rayons de lumière sous les larges et fraîches feuilles du cactus. Un personnage féminin, dont la pose et les traits expriment la langueur et la nonchalance, s'harmonise bien avec la scène.[7]

Le critique se disait déçu de l'atmosphère imprécise dans *A Capri Landscape* mais il en concluait que c'était probablement là la volonté de l'artiste. Il éprouvait aussi des sentiments mitigés à l'égard de *Winnowing,* scène représentant une jeune paysanne travaillant dans les champs au crépuscule. "Le personnage est bien campé", écrivait-il, "et le geste est naturel, mais la présence d'une école à l'arrière-plan a un effet singulier qui ne met pas en valeur le sujet."[8] Il est permis de penser, devant de tels commentaires, que les critiques étaient probablement des artistes d'un certain âge, formés dans la tradition du détail précis et peu enclins à apprécier un style réaliste moins rigide comme celui de Kerr-Lawson. Puisque l'on mentionne des sujets pastoraux et paysans et des effets de lumière, on peut conclure que Kerr-Lawson devait travailler dans le style de l'école de Barbizon.

À l'automne 1881, Kerr-Lawson était à Paris, à l'Académie Julian, où il étudiait sous la direction du peintre de genre classique, Gustave Boulanger, et du portraitiste Jules-Joseph Lefebvre. Ce n'est pas tant le programme d'études comme tel qui lui fut profitable, mais plutôt l'influence du milieu artistique parisien. À la fin des années '70, une forme modifiée de réalisme, duquel on avait éliminé tout aspect radical, avait été assimilée par les académies. En 1882, Courbet se vit finalement accorder une rétrospective à l'École des Beaux Arts. On voyait apparaître une seconde génération de réalistes, quelque peu influencé par l'impressionnisme, et qui avait à sa tête Jules Bastien-Lepage, dont la *Jeanne D'Arc* et le *Mendiant,* exposés aux salons de 1880 et 1881, attiraient nombre d'imitateurs.[9] Le style de Bastien, qui se rapprochait davantage du naturalisme de Degas que du colorisme prismatique de Monet, pouvait être accepté de tous. Chez Bastien et ses disciples, le coup de pinceau se fit plus détendu, la gamme des couleurs s'éclaircit et les sujets non idéalisés furent observés directement. Toutefois, contrairement à Monet, ils continuèrent de s'intéresser à des sujets ayant une signification évidente, à des compositions très structurées et à un certain degré de fini et leurs formes ne s'estompaient jamais dans l'espace. Il y avait alors un autre peintre qui s'attirait des disciples; il s'agissait de l'Américain expatrié James McNeil Whistler, dont les portraits de sa mère, de Thomas Carlyle et de Cicely Alexander créèrent une forte impression lors des Salons de 1883 et 1884. L'oeuvre de Whistler était elle aussi inspirée de Degas, de Velasquez et du *japonisme.* Il avait un style pictural plus libre, ce qui ne l'empêchait pas de s'intéresser à l'équilibre de la composition et aux subtilités des tonalités douces dont il jouait avec un raffinement exquis. Il avait en horreur les sujets réalistes. Durant les années '80 et '90, on vit à travers le monde se répandre le style réaliste-impressionniste qui allait être bientôt abandonné par l'avant-garde du début du siècle. C'est dans ce style que Kerr-Lawson devait se distinguer.

On sait peu de choses au sujet des deux premières années que Kerr-Lawson passa à Paris. Le 20 novembre 1881, Robert Harris, qui visitait la ville, mentionna l'avoir vu.[10] Le 5 décembre, William Blair Bruce, un compatriote de Hamilton qui étudiait lui aussi à l'Académie Julian, écrivait: "Je n'ai pas encore vu Lawson, ce qui ne me manque pas outre mesure."[11] Une lettre de Bruce, datée du 11 décembre 1883, indique que Kerr-Lawson retourna chez lui pour rendre visite à sa famille[12] mais des lettres ultérieures mentionnent qu'il était de retour à Paris en janvier 1884.

Kerr-Lawson s'était déjà à cette époque lié d'amitié avec le peintre canadien William Brymner et avec l'Anglais Frederick William Jackson. Dans une lettre en date du 4 mars, Brymner écrivait à son père:

> Je viens de m'entretenir ce soir avec Jackson et Lawson à propos de nos projets de voyage pour cet été et nous en sommes presque venus à la conclusion qu'il vaudrait mieux aller au Yorkshire qu'en Belgique. Personnellement, je m'y opposais parce que l'endroit est plus coûteux; mais, après avoir calculé libéralement les frais sur les conseils de Jackson qui y a fait plusieurs séjours, nous sommes arrivés au montant de quinze à vingt shillings par semaine, à condition d'y aller à trois ou quatre.[13]

D'après les commentaires ultérieures de Brymner et de Bruce, il semble que Kerr-Lawson ait été un jeune homme charmant mais peu énergique et qui n'avait pas encore de but dans la vie. Le 6 avril, Brymner remarquait:

> Lawson a près de vingt-deux ans et, s'il avait la chance de posséder cinq francs, il dépenserait toute la somme à nous offrir des cigares et du café même s'il savait qu'il ne recevrait pas d'autre argent avant la fin du mois; il ne lui viendrait pas à

---

6. "The Art Gallery," *The Witness* (Montréal), 11 avril 1883.

7. "The Art Exhibition," *The Globe* (Toronto), 26 mai 1883.

8. Ibid.

9. À propos du réalisme de la seconde génération, voir Gabriel P. Weisberg, *The Realist Tradition,* et sur Bastien-Lepage, voir Kenneth McConkey, "The Bouguereau of the Naturalists: Bastien-Lepage and British Art," *Art History,* 1978, pp. 371-82.

10. Lettre de Harris à son père, 20 novembre 1881, documents Harris, Galerie nationale du Canada, Ottawa.

11. Lettre de Bruce à son père, 5 décembre 1881, documents Bruce, Art Gallery of Hamilton, Hamilton.

12. Ibid., 11 décembre 1883.

13. Lettre de Brymner à son père, 4 mars 1884, documents Brymner, Musée McCord, Montréal.

l'idée de s'inquiéter pour les quinze derniers jours. Insouciant dans ses paroles, dans ses actions et dans ses dépenses, c'est pourtant le genre de garçon qu'on ne peut s'empêcher d'aimer. Il peut se donner énormément de peine pour exécuter un tableau et l'achever presque complètement. Pourtant, si vous le revoyez un peu plus tard, il peut aussi bien l'avoir donné à quelqu'un qui l'aurait par hasard admiré. Il y a beaucoup de choses positives en lui et il devrait nous écouter et se mettre sérieusement à travailler. Les idées de tableaux et de compositions ne lui manquent pas, mais il n'a vraiment pas assez de patience.[14]

Plus snob, Blair Bruce racontait:

J'ai vu le jeune Lawson à Paris, un soir, au Café des Ecoles, qui est un endroit où je me contenterais d'aller peut-être une fois l'an. La clientèle y fait vraiment pitié. C'est un gentil garçon qui n'a pas encore de force de caractère, mais il va finir par mûrir, je pense.[15]

La plupart des tableaux exécutés par Kerr-Lawson à Paris ont maintenant disparu. Toutefois, en 1883-1884 il peignit un portrait de Victor Hugo âgé (Collection Mme G. R. Varin, Versailles), une oeuvre sombre, directe et libéralement travaillée. On dit qu'il s'agit là d'un portrait pour lequel Hugo aurait posé, mais cela ne peut être prouvé. Brymner mentionne aussi deux paysages:

l'un inspiré par *L'Oie et les oeufs d'or* de Tennyson (un vieillard debout devant la vieille porte délabrée d'une maison de campagne, avec une vieille femme de même condition, elle aussi debout près de la porte, et à qui il donne une oie. Le vent souffle sur toute la scène et la route boueuse est pleine de flaques d'eau.), l'autre inspiré de Maud Muller.[16]

Alors que le portrait de Hugo est peint à la manière conservatrice du réalisme, les deux paysages étaient probablement dans un style plein-air qui ressemblait à celui de Brymner ou de Bastien-Lepage. Le fait qu'ils soient inspirés de textes littéraires les situe encore davantage sous l'influence de Bastien.

Après un voyage à Brolles, dans la forêt de Fontainebleau, en avril 1884, Brymner, Jackson et Kerr-Lawson revinrent à Paris. Le trente, ils se rendirent au Salon et, le lendemain, ils partirent pour Runswick Bay, au Yorkshire, où ils avaient l'intention de passer l'été. Comme ils n'avaient pas beaucoup d'argent, ils ne s'arrêtèrent pas à Londres et ils ne tardèrent pas à arriver au minuscule village de pêche sis en bordure de la mer du Nord. Ils prirent pension au Sheffield Hotel, se laissèrent pousser la barbe, firent des croquis sur les quais et ne tardèrent pas à s'ennuyer dans ce patelin tranquille. Ils continuèrent à y habiter jusqu'à la fin de novembre, même si leurs seules distractions étaient de jouer au palet et de recevoir quelquefois des visiteurs. On "apprit tout ce qu'il y avait à apprendre sur les petits villages autour de Naples et de Capri et sur les gens que Lawson y avait rencontrés".[17] Brymner peignit plusieurs tableaux, parmi lesquels son fameux *A Wreath of Flowers* (Galerie nationale du Canada). Kerr-Lawson exposa une peinture du pré communal de Runswick lors de l'exposition de 1885 de l'Académie royale des arts du Canada, mais, à part ce tableau, au dire de Brymner, il n'était "pas arrivé à finir quoi que ce soit d'important cet été. Il travaille une pièce jusqu'à un certain point, et d'une manière des plus compétentes, mais il s'en fatigue ensuite et l'abandonne, de sorte qu'elle ne lui rapporte rien."[18] Tard en novembre, le trio se sépara et Kerr-Lawson prit le bateau à Liverpool le vingt-sept. Il devait emporter avec lui un certain nombre de tableaux de Brymner, mais, s'étant trompé dans son horaire, il dut partir plus tôt que prévu et ne put faire la commission. "Comme Lawson est l'homme le plus négligent du monde, peut-être en est-il mieux ainsi...", de commenter Brymner.[19]

Au Canada, Kerr-Lawson demeura avec son frère Andrew qui travaillait à Ottawa pour le Service géologique; il rejoignit plus tard sa famille à Toronto où elle avait emménagé en 1881. Il devint soudain très actif. La première année, il exposa douze huiles et trois aquarelles sous les auspices de l'Académie royale des arts du Canada, de l'Ontario Society of Artists et de l'Association des beaux-arts de Montréal. Le quinze mai et trois novembre respectivement, il fut élu membre des deux premières sociétés. Il ne tarda pas à présenter l'une de ses meilleures oeuvres, *Music, when soft voices die, Vibrates in the memory* (n° 3 du cat.) lors de l'exposition d'hiver de l'O.S.A. Avec son titre poétique emprunté à Shelley, *Music...* aurait pu n'être qu'une oeuvre pré-raphaélique conventionnelle; pourtant, sa composition rappelle de façon frappante la fameuse peinture intitulée *At the Piano* (Taft Museum, Cincinnati, Ohio) que Whistler exécuta en 1858-1859.[20] Il ne s'agit probablement là que d'une coïncidence. *At the Piano* ne fut réellement connu qu'à la fin des années '90. De plus, *Music...* insiste plus que *At the Piano* sur les effets de lumière grâce à ses délicats tons gris argent. Ceux-ci pourraient fort bien provenir des oeuvres plus tardives de Whistler ou de celles de Bastien-Lepage.

C'est en fréquentant les cercles artistiques torontois que Kerr-Lawson fit alors la connaissance du peintre Homer Watson avec qui il devait se lier d'une amitié durable. Pendant plusieurs étés, ils travaillèrent ensemble dans la résidence de Watson à Doon. Il fréquenta également de plus en plus mademoiselle Catherine Adah Muir.[21] Cassy (qu'on appellera plus tard Caterina) était

14. Ibid., 6 avril 1884.

15. Lettre de Bruce à son père, 9 avril 1884, documents Bruce.

16. Lettre de Brymner à son père, 6 avril 1884, documents Brymner.

17. Ibid., 28 mai 1884. "Maud Muller" était un poème de John Greenleaf Whittier.

18. Ibid., 28 novembre 1884.   19. Ibid.

20. L'historique de *At the Piano* apparaît dans Andrew MacLaren Young, *Paintings of James McNeill Whistler* (New Haven: Yale University Press, 1980), vol. 1, n° 24, pp. 8-9.

21. Cassy Muir naquit à Scarborough, Ontario, le 18 novembre 1860. Elle était la fille de John et Eliza Muir. Elle fut élevée par sa grand-mère maternelle à Hamilton et il se peut qu'elle ait connu les Lawson qui fréquentaient eux aussi la Central Presbyterian Church. Au début des années 1870, Eliza Muir épousa David Allan Smith, dont elle eut quatre enfants: Frances, Elizabeth, Adah et William. Devenue veuve en 1884, elle et tous ses enfants accompagnèrent les Watson en Europe en 1887. Ils demeurèrent avec Kerr-Lawson pendant plusieurs années et tous devaient plus tard vivre à Torquay, Devonshire.

une jeune fille intelligente, douée d'un esprit vif et d'une forte personnalité; elle allait contribuer de façon décisive à l'avancement professionnel de Kerr-Lawson.

C'est à peu près à cette époque qu'il peignit le portrait de Cassy (n° 6 du cat.). Au point de vue du style, cette oeuvre est typique de ses premières années et c'est l'une des meilleures qu'il ait jamais exécutées. C'est un portrait en pied, grandeur nature, qui la représente de profil, vêtue d'une robe de bal en soie blanche. Tournée vers la droite, elle pose sur un fond de damas sombre, d'un vert brunâtre. Avec son nez pointu et son menton avancé, Cassy n'est certes pas d'une grande beauté, mais l'aspect contrastant de ses cheveux, de sa peau et de sa robe, et de l'arrière-plan en fait une figure frappante. C'est là l'essence du portrait. Elle repose sur la présence physique de Cassy, particulièrement sur les contrastes et les gradations de tons de la robe et la position même du personnage à l'intérieur du cadre. La pose de profil rend très difficile l'étude psychologique. Cette façon directe et concrète d'aborder le sujet s'inscrit très bien dans la tradition réaliste quoique le souci formel de la tonalité et de la composition, inspiré de Whistler ou de Bastien-Lepage, annonce certainement les tendances décoratives qu'on retrouve dans les oeuvres ultérieures de Kerr-Lawson.

Durant l'année 1886, il s'occupa à peindre des paysages et des tableaux de genre et, occasionnellement, des portraits. En plus des membres de sa famille, il peignit James Smith, de la R.C.A. (n° 4 du cat.) et le révérend Henry James Grasett, doyen de la cathédrale St. James. Ses travaux attiraient maintenant l'attention. Le critique de l'*Ottawa Citizen* mentionnait les "tons tendres" de *Music* . . . et décrivait en ces termes le sujet de *The Orphans:* "trois enfants attablés devant un maigre repas; un chien lève les yeux vers eux."[22] Plus tard la même année, le *Montreal Herald* écrivait que sa peinture *Hoeing Potatoes* représentait une vieille femme et un jeune garçon travaillant aux champs.[23] On trouve une opinion plus critique à son sujet dans une lettre que le marchand de tableaux James Spooner adressait à son ami Homer Watson. Spooner était à l'Imperial and Colonial Exhibition, de Londres, (où le *Wreath of Flowers* de Brymner était exposé), et il répondait à une lettre de Watson:

Ce que tu me dis au sujet de M. Lawson est excellent. Il n'y a guère de poésie en lui et, quoique j'aie toujours cru qu'il était sur le bon chemin, il *doit* aller plus loin. Il possède en effet un certain sens des couleurs, mais cela ne suffit pas. Qu'il se consacre aux choses de base, qu'il y travaille et s'améliore. C'est une étape qu'il doit franchir avant d'être considéré comme un peintre digne de ce nom . . . Il est probable qu'avec beaucoup de travail, M. Lawson parviendra à faire preuve de certaines qualités. Mais il n'y est pas encore parvenu.[24]

Une critique plus élogieuse paraît dans un article du *The Week* en mars 1887. L'auteur, qui rendait compte de l'ouverture d'une nouvelle galerie de Toronto, les Rembrandt Art Rooms, commentait:

C'est sans doute un tableau de M. James Kerr-Lawson de Hamilton qui retient le plus l'attention à la galerie Rembrandt en ce moment. D'ailleurs, quiconque connaît bien le travail de M. Lawson ne sera pas surpris d'apprendre qu'une de ses toiles domine une pièce remplie de tableaux, dont plusieurs sont l'oeuvre d'artistes plus âgés et mieux connus que lui . . . L'oeuvre en question s'éloigne quelque peu de la manière et des choix habituels de sujets de M. Lawson . . . Nous pouvions toujours compter sur lui pour son sens de l'interprétation forte et juste . . . mais il ne nous a pas toujours ni même souvent offert la grâce, la tendresse, la sensibilité naturellement belle et délicate que l'on trouve dans ce dernier tableau. Il s'agit d'une jeune fille au piano. Elle se penche vers l'avant, le visage sur sa musique, les coudes appuyés sur les touches, tandis que, s'abandonnant spontanément au chagrin, elle touche de la main ses yeux pleins de larmes. La jeune fille porte une robe du soir en brocart blanc, dont le drapé et la texture s'avèrent . . . particulièrement bien réussis. C'est là un triomphe de l'artiste.[25]

On ne sait pas où se trouve cette peinture, mais elle est probablement dans la même veine que *Music* . . . et que le portrait de Cassy (n° 6 du cat.) vêtue d'une robe de même genre. Évidemment, il est impossible de savoir à quel point l'auteur de l'article se laisse aller à ses propres sentiments en décrivant le sujet. Le critique de *The Week* retourna aux Rembrandt Rooms en octobre et nota que Kerr-Lawson exposait:

une belle étude de tête, peinte dans la meilleure manière de l'école française, un visage vivant, humain, étonnamment vrai et fidèlement rendu, spécialement en ce qui concerne le nez, les cheveux qui garnissent le front et la justesse implacable de l'affreuse teinte de la peau.[26]

Mais lorsque ce deuxième article parut, Kerr-Lawson s'était déjà découragé quant à son avenir à Toronto et il était parti pour l'étranger. Au cours de l'été, il partit pour l'Europe avec les Watson, les Smith et Cassy Muir. Les Watson s'installèrent près de Londres, les Smith quelque part en France, tandis que Kerr-Lawson étudiait à Paris. Au printemps 1888, il était à Rome où il peignit une petite aquarelle représentant un homme tenant un pic; cette pièce se trouve maintenant à l'Edmonton Art Gallery.

Dès le début de l'été, James était de retour en Grande-Bretagne, où il retrouvait sa mère et son frère Andrew, qui étaient alors en visite là-bas. À leur instigation, et pour limiter ses frais, il décida d'aller à Pittenweem, petit village

22. "Royal Academy Exhibition," *Ottawa Citizen,* 3 février 1886.

23. "Original Drawings," *Montreal Herald,* — octobre 1886.

24. Lettre de Spooner à Watson, 23 juillet 1886, documents Watson, Galerie nationale du Canada, Ottawa.

25. "Art: Mr. Lawson's New Picture," *The Week* (Toronto), 17 mars 1887, p. 257.

26. "Rembrandt House," *The Week,* 20 octobre 1887, p. 760.

de pêche près d'Anstruther, dans le Fifeshire. En juillet, les Watson, les Smith et Cassy l'y rejoignirent.

Quittant leurs chambres louées, ils partaient à l'aventure pour peindre et explorer la campagne. Le soir, ils s'asseyaient et bavardaient. Ils se plaisaient ensemble et Kerr-Lawson et Watson terminèrent tous les deux bon nombre de pièces. Tard en septembre, James partit peindre à Tanger, au Maroc; c'était un endroit très fréquenté en hiver par les artistes européens qui allaient y peindre puisqu'il était facile de s'y rendre, qu'on y trouvait en abondance des motifs exotiques orientaux et que les touristes ne l'avaient pas encore envahi. Cassy et lui allaient revenir maintes fois à Tanger et les sujets marocains constitueraient plus tard une partie importante de son oeuvre. Il employa même une fois un serviteur marocain qu'il fit venir à Londres pour travailler. On sait peu de choses sur son premier séjour au Maroc sinon qu'il fit un voyage dans l'intérieur du pays pour y chasser le sanglier et que, au printemps 1889, il envoya huit peintures marocaines aux expositions de l'O.S.A. et de la R.C.A. Le paysage de petites dimensions intitulé *Mediterranean Coast, Morocco* (n° 9 du cat.) est probablement l'une de ces oeuvres.

Entre temps, tous les autres continuaient d'habiter à Pittenweem. Cassy et Roxa Watson étaient occupées à apprendre le français et à faire l'éloge des ouvrages de Homer à qui voulait les entendre. Roxa écrivait: "Je t'assure que Cassy est la meilleure aide qui soit pour qui vend des peintures. Elle n'y vas pas de main morte, je peux te le dire. Elle ne dit rien de plus que ce qu'elle croit ..."[27] C'est un commentaire qui sera maintes fois répété aussi longtemps que Cassy vivra. Plus tard, la réputation de son mari tiendra pour une large part à ses talents de promotrice.

Toutefois, Homer Watson commençait à être fatigué de Pittenweem et il brûlait d'envie de retourner à Londres. Certains de ses travaux avaient été acceptés au Glasgow Institute of Fine Arts et à la Royal Society of British Artists (desquels Whistler était alors le président) et c'est probablement à l'instar de Watson que Kerr-Lawson fit parvenir ses oeuvres à ces sociétés à partir de 1890.

En mai 1889, tous quittèrent Pittenweem, visitèrent le Salon de Paris puis revinrent à Londres pour l'exposition annuelle de la Royal Academy, ainsi que pour d'autres salons. Il est probable que les Smith passèrent l'été en Allemagne; quant aux Watson, ils s'installèrent à Maidenhead, juste à l'ouest de Londres, où ils demeurèrent avec des parents, les Biggs, avant d'avoir leur propre villa.

Homer renoua avec George Clausen qui demeurait alors tout près et il ne tarda pas à apprendre la gravure à l'eau-forte sous sa direction. C'est sans doute aussi par l'intermédiaire de Watson que Clausen et Kerr-Lawson devinrent vite amis.

Kerr-Lawson retourna au Maroc à la fin d'août, date à laquelle il était déjà fiancé à Cassy Muir. Au début de septembre, ils étaient tous les deux à Maidenhead. "Jim Lawson a l'air un peu plus vieux", écrivit Roxa Watson. "Il porte la barbe, ce qui lui va vraiment mieux. Je ne pense pas . . . que Cassy ait vieilli d'un jour—on lui donne toujours vingt et un ou vingt-deux ans."[28] Le 24 septembre, ils se marièrent au Bureau de l'état civil du village voisin de Cookham; Homer Watson et Edward Biggs leur servirent de témoins. L'après-midi, ils partirent pour Londres et le lendemain ils prirent le train pour l'Écosse. Les Watson étaient étonnés que Cassy ait consenti à épouser James. Phoebe, la soeur de Homer Watson, écrivait: "J'ai oublié de te dire ce que j'entendais en disant que Lawson défiait le destin par son mariage. Les lignes de sa main indiquaient qu'il ne se marierait jamais, tout comme moi; les gens d'ici semblent penser que Mademoiselle Muir aurait mieux fait de ne pas l'épouser, mais à chacun selon son goût, tu ne trouves pas?"[29]

De retour à Pittenweem, Kerr-Lawson connut une période de grande productivité. "D'après les nouvelles qui nous parviennent d'Écosse", remarquait Roxa Watson, "tout le monde semble être heureux là-bas. Jim a déjà envoyé vingt-quatre petits tableaux au Canada et il travaille à en compléter encore bien d'autres. Tu vois l'effet que le mariage a sur certaines gens."[30]

Malheureusement, sa productivité diminua, car en novembre et en décembre il souffrit de pneumonie, ce qui le laissa très abattu. Il écrivait à Watson en janvier.

> . . . je ne sais pas quelle excuse invoquer pour la lettre que je t'écris ce soir. Tu as toujours été bon pour moi, tu m'as toujours traité comme un homme et un frère, et tout ce que j'ai à t'offrir en retour, c'est de t'écrire quand je ne comprends plus rien à rien ou quand j'ai le cafard. Je t'ai envoyé une photo du tableau que j'ai envoyé à Glasgow; c'était un geste aussi inexcusable que l'est ma lettre de ce soir. Ce tableau, qui mesure 60 pouces par 40, est une bien vilaine chose. Je ne sais guère pourquoi je l'ai peint, mais je sais que je ne l'aurais pas fait si j'avais été riche. J'ai maintenant sur mon chevalet un tableau plus petit qui traite d'un sujet triste mais qui est mieux traité que les cueilleurs de pommes de terre. Il s'agit de l'intérieur de la boutique de Millar: il y a un vieux type qui construit un petit cercueil blanc en présence d'une petite fille qui, en le regardant faire, serre sur sa poitrine sa poupée aux cheveux blonds, alors qu'elle sent monter en elle la première pointe de l'instinct maternel.

---

27. Lettre de Roxa à Phoebe Watson, 10 février 1889, dans Frank E. Page, *Homer Watson*, p. 144.

28. Lettre de Roxa à Phoebe, 7 octobre 1889, documents Watson.

29. Lettre de Phoebe à Roxa, 3 décembre 1889.

30. Lettre de Roxa à Phoebe, 30 octobre 1889.

Puisque c'est là le sujet et que cela demande, je pense, une autre excuse, je t'affirme, mon cher Watson, que l'effort requis pour introduire un élément d'intérêt dans mon travail, m'a presque totalement vanné. Pourquoi nous faut-il faire reposer une belle peinture sur un élément dramatique ou moral... En fait, non seulement elle n'en a pas besoin, mais elle est plus réussie sans cela...

Oh Watson, comme le monde est triste et déprimant l'hiver en Écosse quand on manque d'argent et que les lettres d'amitié qui nous parviennent de temps en temps, par-ci par-là, ne servent qu'à intensifier ce sentiment d'isolement... Inutile de te dire, mon cher Homer que la présente est le fruit d'un moment de cafard.[31]

Watson lui avait envoyé quelques-unes de ses récentes eaux-fortes et Kerr-Lawson exprimait ensuite son enthousiasme à leur égard. "J'aimerais infiniment", écrivit-il,

tailler une plaque avec toi, et mieux encore, avoir le plaisir d'en imprimer une. À l'avenir, pour certaines de tes expériences, Watson, essaie autant que possible de travailler davantage la ligne pour la ligne, en vertu du principe que le blanc est aussi précieux que le noir, en ce sens qu'un accent sombre ici et là sur un fond clair peut être très significatif. Tonnerre! J'en ai tellement à te dire sur le métier. Ces remarques fragmentaires sont presque une impertinence. Quel est le prix du cuivre?[32]

Kerr-Lawson se lança activement dans la gravure à l'eau-forte et la lithographie après 1900; mais c'est dans cette lettre qu'il manifeste pour la première fois son intérêt pour les estampes.

Pendant les années '80, plusieurs artistes britanniques s'étaient mis à graver à la pointe sèche ou au crayon. En suivant l'exemple de Whistler, ils firent de l'art de l'estampe un véritable mouvement qui devait se prolonger jusque dans les années '20. On ne connaît que quelques-unes des premières estampes de Kerr-Lawson. L'un de ses neveux possède une petite eau-forte qui représente une femme d'âge moyen portant un bonnet.[33] La Leeds City Art Gallery acquit en 1893 une estampe en couleurs du temple de Vesta à Rome.

On sait peu de choses des activités de Kerr-Lawson durant les quelques années qui suivirent. Au printemps 1890, Watson et lui travaillèrent de nouveau ensemble à Pittenweem, plus tard la même année, on le retrouve dans le Kirkcudbrightshire (dans le sud-ouest de l'Écosse) où il exécute au pastel une belle pièce intitulée *Poor Sue* (n° 13 du cat.) qui représente une fille de ferme. Il voulait voyager de nouveau en Italie, mais on ne saurait dire s'il y est allé.

Il est probable qu'il passa quelque temps à Londres car il se lia d'une amitié solide avec George Frederick Watts, le vénéré doyen des peintres victoriens de Grande-Bretagne.

Watts présenta Kerr-Lawson à ses amis et il lui permit même d'utiliser son atelier de Londres pour y tenir une exposition de peintures qui allait avoir du succès.[34] C'était probablement en 1899 car, plus tard la même année, Watts, dans une entrevue accordée à la revue *Saturday Night*, affirmait que Kerr-Lawson était un peintre d'avenir. "M. J. Kerr-Lawson", débutait l'article,

ce jeune artiste canadien... dont on a dit beaucoup de bien dans plusieurs revues, devrait-il connaître finalement le succès artistique qui lui permettrait de faire carrière comme peintre? C'est la question que nous avons posée cet été à Sir James Watt [sic], R.A., lorsque nous l'avons rencontré chez lui. 'Oui, bien sûr qu'il réussira,' répondit celui qui fait autorité en la matière, 'car il possède au moins deux avantages essentiels au succès: il a une bonne épouse et il est intelligent.'[35]

En 1891, Kerr-Lawson et les Smith demeuraient à Oxgang House, une grande villa qu'ils avaient louée à Kirkintilloch, dans la banlieue nord-est de Glasgow. Ils y restèrent environ trois ans. Le peu que l'on sache d'eux durant cette période provient d'une lettre adressée à Cassy, plusieurs années plus tard par un certain Harry Swan, qui leur avait rendu visite à Oxgang House.

'Il me revient à l'esprit', écrivait-il, maints souvenirs oubliés... mes séjours agréables à Kirkintilloch... la présence de ton mari, de ta mère et de deux soeurs et, je crois, d'un petit frère qui était passionné par les trains miniatures—votre départ pour le Maroc et votre retour d'Afrique avec les fruits de ce voyage: des peintures où l'éclat du soleil me réchauffait le coeur... des marches avec ton mari au clair de lune entre les vieux murs de votre jardin.[36]

En s'établissant à Kirkintilloch, Kerr-Lawson s'intégrait à la Glasgow School, laquelle était alors, avec la Newlyn School et le New English Art Club, le point de ralliement des jeunes peintres de plein-air britanniques. Inspirés par l'École de Barbizon, Courbet, l'École de la Haye, Bastien-Lepage, Whistler et les impressionnistes, les "Glasgow Boys" (ayant à leur tête James Guthrie, W. Y. Macgregor, John Lavery, E. A. Hornell et George Henry) peignaient alors leurs oeuvres les plus importantes et ils constituaient une force certaine au sein de l'art britannique et sa présence devait se sentir bien avant dans la période édouardienne. Lavery et Henry, en particulier, entretinrent une amitié durable avec Kerr-Lawson. De 1894 à 1898, Kerr-Lawson vécut de façon intermittente à Glasgow même. Il exposa au Royal Glasgow Institute of Fine Arts mais c'est dans une galerie inconnue de Glasgow qu'il tint sa première exposition individuelle.[37] C'était aussi la première fois que son nom apparaissait dans une revue d'importance, *The Magazine of Art,* laquelle parlait favorablement du tableau intitulé *The Ploughman*[38] qu'il

---

31. Lettre de Kerr-Lawson à Homer Watson, 11 janvier 1890, dans Jane Van Every, *With Faith, Ignorance and Delight,* pp. 50-51 et Muriel Miller, *Homer Watson,* p. 39.

32. Ibid.

33. Dr. Douglas Kerr-Lawson, Waterloo.

34. Procès-verbal de la réunion du Canadian Art Club, 1912, dossier des coupures de presse sur Kerr-Lawson, bibliothèque du Musée des beaux-arts de l'Ontario, Toronto.

35. Jean Grant, "Studio and Gallery," *Saturday Night,* 30 décembre 1889, p. 9.

36. Lettre de Swan à Caterina, 20 mars 1947, archives de la famille Lawson, Andover, Mass.

37. "Scottish Painter of Picturesque," *Glasgow Herald,* 22 février 1949.

38. "The Chronicle of Art: Exhibitions," *The Magazine of Art,* avril 1893, p. xxvii.

avait présenté à l'Institute. Aujourd'hui, peu de gens à Glasgow savent qui est Kerr-Lawson.[39]

En plus de séjourner au Maroc tel que déjà mentionné, Kerr-Lawson passa la plus grande partie des années '90 en France, en Espagne et en Italie. Plusieurs artistes britanniques vinrent à Paris pour le Salon de 1893; c'est à ce moment que Kerr-Lawson rencontra Whistler à son atelier de la Rue de Bac et qu'il se promena avec lui dans son jardin, tout en discutant de l'impact qu'avait eu le tableau *The Buccaneers,* une oeuvre du jeune Frank Brangwyn.[40] Nul ne sait avec certitude quand ni comment Kerr-Lawson devint un des intimes de Whistler. C'est peut-être par l'intermédiaire de Watson, de ses amis de Glasgow ou de son frère Edward. Edward travaillait pour le compte de William Heinemann qui était l'éditeur de Whistler en même temps que son ami. Heinemann donnait des soupers qui sont restés célèbres et c'est probablement lors d'une de ces soirées que Kerr-Lawson établit des liens d'amitié avec l'écrivain et potier William de Morgan, avec le romancier Maurice Hewlett et avec le couple de journalistes-illustrateurs Elizabeth et Joseph Pennell.

En juin 1893, il était de nouveau à Tanger, où il se lia également d'amitié avec Frank Brangwyn. Des années plus tard, il se souvint de leur rencontre en peignant le portrait de Brangwyn (n° 77 du cat.) Il écrivait à ce sujet:

> Il y a plusieurs années, José Tapiro me présenta à Frank Brangwyn à Tanger. Brangwyn, contrairement à moi, ne portait pas la djellaba, pourtant je viens de le peindre dans l'habit d'un chef maure parce qu'il me semble que c'est ainsi que je me souviens de lui, avec tout le Maroc comme fond de scène. Je parle du Maroc que l'on rejoignait en traversant de Tarifa à Tanger en felouque, avec un équipage de contre-bandiers transportant vers le Riff du tabac, du genièvre hollandais et des fusils, bien avant que la Compagnie Générale Transatlantique ait rendu le pays aussi sûr qu'un lieu de vacances pour écoliers![41]

Pendant la plus grande partie de l'année suivante, il travailla en Espagne, spécialement à Madrid. En plus de se consacrer à son oeuvre, il aida son frère Edward à compiler un guide Heinemann du Prado. C'est là qu'il étudia les chefs-d'oeuvre des maîtres vénitiens, et il en copia même quelques-uns. Maurice Hewlett, dans une de ses lettres, affirme l'avoir trouvé "aux prises avec l'âme du Titien", probablement en train d'exécuter une copie de la *Mise au tombeau,* aujourd'hui perdue.[42]

L'enthousiasme des deux amis pour la peinture véni-tienne s'inscrivait dans une tendance générale de plus en plus marquée. La parution de *Modern Painters* et *The Stones of Venice* de Ruskin ainsi que celle de l'essai de Walter Pater intitulé "The School of Georgione" avait suscité l'intérêt. Des ouvrages aussi érudits que le *Life and Times of Titian* de Crowe et Cavalcaselle et le *Venetian Painters of the Renaissance* de Bernard Berenson avaient ensuite accentué cette orientation. Cette tendance marquerait éventuellement toute une génération de jeunes artistes, spécialement ceux qui étaient muralistes.

De retour d'Espagne, Kerr-Lawson se retrouva à Paris à la fin de l'été 1894. William Heinemann, qui préparait une édition du Journal des Goncourt, le rencontra par hasard et lui commanda un portrait du poète symboliste Paul Verlaine.

> 'Bon Dieu!' s'exclama-t-il, 'vous êtes justement l'homme qu'il me faut,' et il me jeta dans un taxi et me conduisit chez Blanchet, rue Bonaparte, où je me procurai diverses fourni-tures, après quoi nous nous précipitâmes à la mansarde de Verlaine. Nous y trouvâmes Verlaine assis appuyé sur des oreillers, avec ses pommettes saillantes, ses yeux bleus en amande, son nez aux narines très larges, sa barbe jaunâtre embroussaillée et ses quelques mèches de cheveux blonds. Une atmosphère de charme vraiment indescriptible semblait émaner de lui alors qu'il nous souhaitait la bienvenue d'une voix douce et caressante. Il parlait et plaisantait en un anglais singulièrement charmant, car il connaissait à merveille la littérature victorienne et il émaillait sa conversation de citations de Tennyson, De Quincey, Shelley et Keats.[43]

Le dessin au fusain exécuté lors de cette séance (Collection de Mme G. R. Varin, Versailles) servit de modèle au portrait peint à l'huile (n° 14 du cat.) qui se trouve maintenant au Fitzwilliam Museum de Cambridge. C'est un portrait franc et d'une grande justesse psychologique mais moins beau et de moindre qualité formelle que les autres portraits exécutés par Kerr-Lawson; ce tableau contraste vivement avec celui d'Eugène Carrière qui fait de Verlaine un véritable poète visionnaire.

Il se peut que les Kerr-Lawson aient visité l'Angleterre à l'automne mais, en novembre, ils étaient à Florence, qui allait devenir bientôt leur second foyer. En s'y installant, ils suivaient l'exemple d'un aîné, le Canadien Antoine-Sébastien Falardeau (1822-1889), célèbre en son temps pour ses copies des vieux maîtres. À leur arrivée, ils rencontrèrent Mme Janet Ross, écrivaine et grande dame de la colonie anglo-florentine. Mme Ross se rappelait par la suite que:

> À la fin de l'automne deux amis de 'Signor' [George Frederick Watts], M. et Mme Kerr-Lawson, arrivèrent à Florence et me remirent une lettre dans laquelle on me demandait de faire tout en mon pouvoir pour les aider. Ils nous ont plu tout de suite, tant le mari que la femme, mais, comme 'Signor' ne mentionnait pas quelle profession M. Kerr-Lawson exerçait ni ce que je devais faire pour eux, j'étais

39. Il est mentionné brièvement dans James Caw, *Scottish Painting Past and Present,* p. 389.

40. William de Belleroche, *Brangwyn's Pilgrimage,* p. 167.

41. "A Famous Royal Academician as a Moorish Chief: Mr. Frank Brangwyn," *The Illustrated London News,* 10 octobre 1931.

42. Lettre de Hewlett à Kerr-Lawson, 14 décembre 1893, archives de la famille Lawson.

43. James Kerr-Lawson, "A Newly 'Discovered' Portrait of Verlaine," *Apollo,* mai 1939, p. 262.

plutôt perplexe. À la fin, je le lui demandai de but en blanc, à sa grande surprise, je pense, car il croyait que 'Signor' m'avait dit qu'il était un artiste. Ils s'installèrent à Settignano jusqu'à ce qu'ils se trouvent un charmant petit coin, la vieille villa qui avait déjà appartenu au père de Boccaccio, à Corbignano. Nous devinrent des amis intimes et Kerr-Lawson fit un portrait admirable de Henry. [Henry James Ross, son mari, n° 16 du cat.][44]

Les Kerr-Lawson allaient demeurer pendant plus de quarante ans dans cette Casa di Boccaccio mentionée par Mme Ross. C'était certainement plus qu'une "vieille villa". L'écrivain Edward Hutton, un ami qui eut l'occasion d'y résider, la décrivit en ces termes:

une maison . . . avec deux loggias enfouies dans les roses et un petit oratoire dédié à la Madone des Epées. La Casa di Boccaccio, voilà comment on appelle l'endroit . . . Peut-être, si le propriétaire vous en fait la politesse . . . irez-vous flâner quelque peu dans le jardin et voir la magnifique cour avec son vieux puits et les fresques en ruine que l'on peut encore deviner sur les murs de ce qui était autrefois la tour ainsi que les inscriptions abîmées.[45]

Les Kerr-Lawson ne tardèrent pas à avoir beaucoup d'amis à Florence. Le plus illustre d'entre eux était leur voisin, le jeune Américain spécialiste de l'art de la Renaissance, Bernard Berenson. Ils se rencontrèrent vers 1897, par l'intermédiaire de Janet Ross, et devinrent bientôt des amis intimes. Dès le printemps, Berenson et son épouse, Mary, posèrent pour Kerr-Lawson qui fit d'eux de petits portraits au crayon (Collection Berenson, Florence, pour le premier; localisation inconnue pour le second). Ils faisaient souvent la navette entre leurs villas respectives et lorsque Berenson et Mary s'épousèrent officiellement, en décembre 1900, Kerr-Lawson et Caterina se trouvaient parmi les amis intimes invités à la cérémonie. Or Berenson commençait à s'enrichir et il aimait à venir en aide à ses amis moins fortunés.

Les Kerr-Lawson, dont la situation précaire, dans leur villa de Fiesole, inquiétait depuis longtemps Berenson, furent parmi les premiers à bénéficier de son aide. Il leur indiqua des tableaux qu'on pouvait acheter pour une somme dérisoire. L'un acquis à Venise pour £15, fut vendu à un riche marchand de Glasgow pour £350, ce qui "les éloignait d'autant de la pauvreté", au dire même de Mary. Un autre, comme l'apprit Mary, permit un profit encore plus spectaculaire. Achetée pour £1, il se vendit pour £900. Ainsi lancé, Kerr-Lawson s'établit à son compte comme marchand de tableaux et ne dépendit plus pour survivre de la vente toujours incertaine de ses propres oeuvres.[46]

Kerr-Lawson continuera toute sa vie à être marchand de tableaux.

À la fin des années '90, les Kerr-Lawson se déplacèrent, selon les saisons, entre Florence et Glasgow, avec de courts séjours à Londres. Le meilleur compte rendu individuel de leurs activités se trouve dans certaines lettres de Maurice Hewlett. En février 1897, il écrivit à Kerr-Lawson qui avait encore une fois souffert de pneumonie et se trouvait alors à Dumfries:

Jamais je n'ai vu la Providence affirmer aussi poliment, mais fermement, qu'un homme ayant tes qualités de tête et de coeur et, ajouterais-je, tes poumons, ne devrait pas vivre en Écosse, alors que Londres t'attend impatiemment.

J'espère que tu ne passeras pas outre à cet avertissement qui me semble sans équivoque. Les îles Canaries, c'est très bien pour les Canaries, et ton Dumfries peut bien convenir à Carlyle et à sa philosophie de croque-mort, mais Londres est le lieu idéal pour un homme de ta sensibilité—on y est stimulé sans excès et amusé sans débauche. Et si j'ajoute que ce serait là pour toi une occasion unique d'étudier à volonté les vieux maîtres et même ma tête (j'y collerai un buste et des épaules pour le seul plaisir de figurer près du torse de Farnèse) tu te rendras compte sans plus tarder que tu t'entêtes erronément et que tu ne sais pas voir tes propres intérêts.[47]

Plusieurs années plus tard, Kerr-Lawson se rendit finalement aux arguments de Hewlett et il s'installa donc dans la métropole. En 1898, les deux amis s'entretinrent des illustrations que Kerr-Lawson faisait pour une nouvelle édition de *Earthwork Out of Tuscany* de Hewlett. Elle fut publiée par Dent en 1899 et elle suscita une abondante correspondance. Il s'agit évidemment de lettres d'affaires, mais les deux amis y parlent aussi de se rencontrer en Italie au printemps et les Hewlett se déclarent enchantés du portrait que Kerr-Lawson vient de faire de leur fils Cecco (Mme Dorothy G. Hewlett, Tauranga, Nouvelle-Zélande). Lorsque parut *Earthwork,* Hewlett devait écrire dans sa préface:

Une chose est claire: quoi qu'on puisse dire de mes illustrations, M. Lawson a animé les siennes de l'esprit même des endroits qui nous sont chers à tous. J'y vais d'un commentaire à sa suite et j'en suis fort aise, car je sais que vous m'etendriez d'autant plus volontiers qu'il aura déjà su captiver votre regard.[48]

En mai 1898, Kerr-Lawson participa, à Londres, à la première exposition de l'International Society of Sculptors, Painters and Gravers. Il y fit voir une vue de Venise pleine d'ambiance, (on ne sait pas où se trouve cette oeuvre mais la Witt Library en possède une photographie) et qui, selon la presse, représentait "une oeuvre typique" de l'école de Glasgow.[49] L'International Society, mise sur pied par John Lavery et présidée par Whistler, était l'un des centres d'exposition les plus avancés de son époque

44. Janet Ross, *The Fourth Generation,* p. 338.

45. Edward Hutton, *Country Walks about Florence,* p. 11.

46. Ernest Samuels, *Bernard Berenson: The Making of a Connoisseur,* p. 310. La citation provient du journal personnel de Mary Berenson, 3 novembre 1899.

47. Lettre de Hewlett à Kerr-Lawson, 15 février 1897, archives de la famille Lawson.

48. Maurice Hewlett, *Earthwork out of Tuscany,* vol. 1, p. x.

49. George Sauter, "The International Society of Painters, Sculptors and Gravers," *The Studio,* août 1898, p. 110.

et elle jouait un rôle important dans l'établissement de relations entre les artistes anglais et français en présentant les oeuvres de Monet, Sisley, Rodin, Bonnard, Toulouse-Lautrec et Cézanne. Kerr-Lawson resta membre de la Society jusque dans les années 1920. James Wilson Morrice fut le seul autre Canadien à en être membre.

En février 1899, Whistler se rendit à Rome pour le mariage de William Heinemann. Sur le chemin du retour, il s'arrêta à Florence, où les Kerr-Lawson lui offrirent l'hospitalité. Ils visitèrent la fameuse salle des autoportraits de la Galerie des Offices; Whistler y rendit un vibrant hommage à Velasquez mais il fut ignoré par l'administration du musée.[50] Après la mort de Whistler, on tenta d'obtenir un de ses autoportraits pour l'ajouter à la collection: on n'y parvint pas.

Les Kerr-Lawson quittèrent l'Écosse pour Londres vers 1900. Ils trouvèrent à se loger au coeur du quartier artistique de Chelsea, au 4 Turner Studios sur Glebe Place. Ils allaient y demeurer pendant plus de cinquante ans.

Glebe Place était une petite rue où se trouvaient de très nombreux studios. Pendant les années '90, des hommes célèbres y avaient tour à tour habité, comme Walter Sickert, William Rothenstein, Charles Conder et James Guthrie. À l'époque des Kerr-Lawson, elle abritait les sculpteurs Derwent Wood et Havard Thomas, les peintres George Henry, Glyn Philpot et George Washington Lambert, le photographe et baron Adolphe de Meyer, le danseur Anton Dolin et l'architecte de style art nouveau, Charles Rennie MacIntosh, qui a conçu plusieurs des maisons qui s'y trouvent.

Avec un revenu stable, une résidence fixe et un cercle d'amis toujours plus grand, Kerr-Lawson s'épanouit enfin comme peintre; alors commença pour lui une période des plus fécondes, qui allait durer jusqu'après la Première Guerre mondiale. Il fréquentait maintenant plus assidûment les Pennel, les de Morgan, les Hewlett et George Clausen. Vers 1904, il entra au Chelsea Arts Club et, en novembre 1907, à l'Art Workers Guild. Il demeura un ami intime de Watts et de Whistler et il lui arriva de séjourner à Limnerslease, maison que Watts possédait dans le Surrey, pour y faire des gravures à l'eau-forte et des estampes en couleurs "compliments à la Signor."[51]

En avril 1903, Kerr-Lawson tint une exposition de ses *Petits Paysages d'Italie,* aux Dowdeswell Galleries de Londres. Ces quelque quarante paysages avaient été peints principalement en mars et en avril 1902 alors qu'il voyageait à travers l'Italie avec Maurice Hewlett.[52] Hewlett écrivit une brève introduction pour le catalogue publié par les Dowdeswell Galleries. Dans ses remarques, il faisait justement allusion à ce tour d'Italie:

> Pour peindre ce pays, il fallait non seulement à l'artiste des couleurs et des toiles, mais il lui fallait encore prendre son temps, regarder d'un coeur léger l'endroit choisi et en faire ressortir le cachet; il lui fallait aimer ces travailleurs et surtout éprouver du respect et de la gratitude pour les gens les plus simples, les plus honnêtes et les meilleurs d'Europe, ainsi que pour leur pays patiné par le temps et usé par les intempéries. Je n'ai pas qualité pour vanter les mérites de l'oeuvre de M. Kerr-Lawson, quoiqu'ils me paraissent considérables, mais je me permettrai de dire que personne ne connaît l'Italie plus que lui ni ne l'aime plus sincèrement.[53]

Seuls quelques-uns des ouvrages exposés à cette occasion peuvent maintenant être identifiés avec certitude. Y figuraient probablement les deux vues de Sienne qui furent reproduites avec un compte rendu de l'exposition et les deux paysages vénitiens qui servirent d'illustration à un article que Kerr-Lawson écrivit sur la peinture en détrempe. Les critiques accueillirent ses oeuvres avec respect. Le journal *The Times* les trouva "extrêmement accomplies" et *The Magazine of Art* les décrivit ainsi:

> ce sont là des exemples d'un art sincère mis au service de sujets vraiment bien choisis. C'est un artiste [de poursuivre le critique] au goût extrêmement juste et son travail possède des qualités certaines quant à la conception et à l'interprétation. Bien . . . qu'il ait abordé des thèmes auxquels bien d'autres peintres se sont intéressés, il les a traités de façon si pertinente et si personnelle qu'il a réussi à les rendre étonnamment attrayants.[55]

Ce fut *The Athenaeum* qui publia l'analyse la plus détaillée de cette exposition. Après avoir mentionné le fait que Kerr-Lawson était peu connu en Angleterre et qu'il avait vécu à l'étranger, le journal louait sa manière directe d'aborder un sujet et surtout son choix perspicace des coloris tout en faisant remarquer l'évidente sympathie du peintre pour ses motifs. Quelques ouvrages, tels que l'*Arno at Pisa* (nº 23) étaient imposants et exprimaient des états d'âme puissamment sentis.[56]

Kerr-Lawson exécuta également, à peu près à la même époque, une série de paysages de la Grèce ou de la Sicile. Dans une lettre envoyée à Elizabeth Pennell en novembre 1904, Caterina déclare que son mari "vient de recevoir une commande d'un millionnaire, un certain M. Loeb de New York, ce qui nous amènera peut-être en Sicile ou en Grèce au printemps, car c'est là le genre de paysage que Loeb a en vue."[57] Le M. Loeb auquel elle fait allusion est probablement James Loeb, banquier à la retraite et philanthrope, qui avait étudié à Harvard avec Berenson et qui avait fondé la Loeb Classical Library dont Heinemann

---

50. E. R. et J. Pennell, *The Life of James McNeill Whistler,* pp. 360-61; Pennell, *The Whistler Journal,* pp. 45-47.

51. Lettre de Kerr-Lawson à Joseph Pennell, non datée, documents Pennell, Library of Congress, Washington, D.C.

52. Maurice Hewlett, *The Letters,* pp. 66-71.

53. *Little Landscapes of Italy,* Dowdeswell Galleries, Londres, avril 1903.

54. "Minor Art Exhibitions," *The Times,* 14 avril 1903.

55. "London Exhibitions," *The Magazine of Art,* juin 1903, pp. 422-23.

56. "Messrs. Dowdeswell's Gallery," *The Athenaeum,* 11 avril 1903, p. 473.

57. Lettre de Caterina à Elizabeth Pennell, 26 novembre 1904, documents Pennell.

était l'éditeur. On ignore si cette commande a été exécutée et ce qu'il en est advenu.

Vers 1903, Kerr-Lawson se lança dans une carrière de peintre muraliste. Il était intéressé à la chose depuis longtemps et il s'était longuement entretenu de ce sujet avec Watts. En novembre 1901, ils avaient été tous deux membres fondateurs de la Society of Painters in Tempera (maintenant la Society of Mural Painters).[58]

En Grande-Bretagne, c'était depuis les années 1840 que l'on cherchait à remettre la peinture murale au rang des arts décoratifs majeurs. Toutefois, en l'absence d'une tradition bien vivante, les styles et les techniques en vigueur ne permettaient guère d'atteindre à un niveau artistique élevé. Étant donné le coût important des murales, peu de gens pouvaient se permettre d'en commander et celles qui furent exécutées ne représentaient que des efforts isolés. Watts en avait fait plusieurs mais il avait ensuite abandonné cette activité. Toutefois, l'importance accordée aux murales dans le schéma décoratif global faisait partie intégrante de la philosophie du mouvement des Arts et Métiers. À la fin des années '90, ces rêves de renouveau semblaient devoir se réaliser. La prospérité et la confiance en soi amenèrent un boom dans la construction. Les peintres muralistes amélioraient leur style et leur technique en étudiant les réalisations du moyen âge et de la Renaissance. L'historicisme allait dominer ce renouveau jusqu'à son déclin, dans les années 1920. Les peintres qui s'inscrivaient dans la tradition classique insistaient sur l'illusion spatiale, le clair-obscur et la forme bien modelée tandis que ceux qui travaillaient dans la tradition du moyen âge mettaient l'accent sur la nature plate de la surface du mur en utilisant de grandes formes simples, des contours nets, des compositions cadencées et des surfaces légères et mates. Kerr-Lawson allait s'inscrire dans ces deux traditions. Si son inspiration était classique, il n'en recherchait pas moins l'absence de relief, sans toutefois verser dans l'archaïsme. Il ressemblait en cela à ses amis Brangwyn et Clausen et à certains des disciples de Puvis de Chavannes. Toutefois, contrairement à celui de Brangwyn, le style de Kerr-Lawson était sobre et n'avait guère l'opulence et la vigueur qui avaient rendu Brangwyn si populaire.

La première série de murales commandée à Kerr-Lawson, la plus importante aussi, devait servir à la décoration de Stoke Rochford Hall, demeure que Christopher Hatton Turnor possédait au Lincolnshire. Turnor était né à Toronto où il avait passé son enfance; après avoir reçu son diplôme d'Oxford en 1896, il avait étudié l'architecture et s'était établi dans le Surrey. Il se lia d'amitié avec son voisin, George Watts et, en 1903-1904, il conçut La Watts Gallery qui fut érigée sur la propriété du peintre.[59] C'est là qu'il rencontra Kerr-Lawson. Turnor venait d'hériter de vastes domaines ancestraux situés dans le Lincolnshire et il tentait d'y implanter des méthodes modernes et efficaces d'exploitation agricole. L'entreprise allait lui valoir une réputation de réformateur agricole et social; il publia à ce propos cinq livres importants.

Kerr-Lawson peignit sur toiles ses murales puis on les encastra dans les panneaux muraux de plusieurs salons de style Louis XV, où elles formaient des ensembles complets. C'était de vastes perspectives de villes italiennes, des grisailles de paysans et d'animaux ou des collages de papier de forme ovale représentant des paysages et des tableaux de genre. On en exposa une douzaine à l'Alpine Club Gallery en juin-juillet 1906 et cela lui mérita le surnom de "Canaletto anglais."[60] Le critique du *Times* insista particulièrement sur le fait que les panneaux devaient être considérés globalement plutôt qu'individuellement. "Ainsi perçus", écrivait-il,

> ces panneaux aux tons sobres, peints avec finesse, présentent une apparence presque sans relief par rapport aux murs blancs et ils créent un effet décoratif admirable, intéressant, reposant et discret. Dans l'ensemble, leur composition est large et simple, car c'est justement vers la composition plutôt que vers l'ambiance que l'artiste a porté tous ses efforts. En même temps, leur couleur est pure et les panneaux sont si habilement disposés les uns par rapport aux autres qu'ils se mettent mutuellement en valeur. Le mur qui se trouve à gauche du visiteur en entrant est particulièrement remarquable par une disposition qui permet une subtile gradation.[61]

Les panneaux de Stoke Rochford restèrent en place jusqu'en 1978; ils furent alors vendus chez Christie par la nièce de Turnor et semés aux quatre vents. On ne connaît la localisation que de quelques-uns. Ils se révélèrent une source importante de motifs pour les ouvrages ultérieurs de Kerr-Lawson et on en tira des copies peintes, des lithographies et des affiches.

À les voir maintenant hors contexte, il est difficile d'évaluer les panneaux en tant qu'ensemble. Ils ont en commun la couleur, les proportions et une même façon de silhouetter les édifices sur un fond de ciel. La répétition de ces éléments contribuait certainement à accentuer l'unité de l'ensemble et à faire ressortir la nature plate inhérente à la surface du mur. Au point de vue du sujet, de la précision et de la composition, la comparaison avec les ouvrages de Canaletto est valable. Il reste que les panneaux de Kerr-Lawson sont peints de façon beaucoup plus large et plus simple. Comparativement à ses ouvrages antérieurs, ils sont moins réalistes,

---

58. Les autres membres fondateurs étaient Walter Crane, William Holman Hunt et Joseph Southall. Parmi les premiers membres de renom se trouvaient Edwin Austin Abbey, Robert Anning Bell et Sir William Blake Richmond.

59. Mary Watts, *George Frederick Watts*, vol. 2, pp. 305-07.

60. L'origine du nom est incertaine mais il est répété à maintes reprises plus tard.

61. "Exhibitions," *The Times*, 11 juin 1906.

plus décoratifs et historiques. Toutefois, quoique modifié, le réalisme demeure toujours présent et l'on y trouve encore un intérêt pour les compositions puissantes et les effets de lumière et de tonalité.

Peu après son exposition à l'Alpine Club Gallery, Kerr-Lawson reçut une commande du baron Aldenham qui désirait des perspectives de Londres pour une petite pièce octogonale d'Aldenham House, près d'Elstrée, dans le Hertfordshire. Aldenham,[62] qui avait posé deux fois pour Watts, était un banquier, un érudit et un collectionneur d'art; il avait vu les panneaux de Stoke Rochford et il voulait quelque chose du même genre. Kerr-Lawson et lui s'entendirent pour choisir sept édifices historiques, principalement de Wren et Gibbs. Il s'agissait de l'édifice des Horse Guards du pont de Londres, de St. Clement Danes, de Hyde Park Corner, de la cathédrale St. Paul, de St. Margaret, de Westminster et de St. Martin-in-the-Fields. Ces perspectives furent également peintes sur toile puis encastrées dans les panneaux des murs. Le plus grand panneau mesurait 84″ x 56″ et le plus petit 36″ x 35″. Kerr-Lawson aborda ces sujets de la même façon qu'il l'avait fait dans les panneaux de Stoke Rochford. La plupart de ces perspectives sont vues sous un éclairage net et uniforme; leur composition est juste et des tons similaires de gris perle et de gris bleu contribuent à l'unité de l'ensemble. Ces pièces inspirèrent elles aussi des lithographies et des affiches.

Lord Aldenham mourut en 1907, alors que l'on était à installer les panneaux; son fils, l'Hon. Vicary Gibbs, demanda à Kerr-Lawson d'exécuter un bas-relief commémoratif en marbre représentant la tête du défunt. Kerr-Lawson n'était certainement pas sculpteur.[63] Le bas-relief a été perdu; toutefois, l'actuel Lord Aldenham s'en rappelle comme d'une "pièce incroyablement lugubre."[64] Quant aux panneaux, ils demeurèrent en place pendant plusieurs années mais ils furent ensuite déplacés et ils sont maintenant en possession des descendants d'Aldenham, à Londres.

En 1907-1908 Kerr-Lawson s'adonna de façon plus soutenue à la lithographie. Il s'intéressait depuis longtemps à la fabrication des estampes mais on ne sait pas grand-chose des pièces qu'il aurait pu faire. La lithographie avait toujours été le parent pauvre des arts graphiques. On la considérait comme un procédé de reproduction strictement commercial qui n'aurait en soi que très peu de véritables possibilités artistiqes. Les marchands de tableaux et les collectionneurs ne s'y intéressaient à peu près pas. Durant les années '80, Whistler avait commencé à faire des lithographies et, durant les années '90, quelques artistes plus jeunes avaient suivi son

exemple. En France, la lithographie artistique connaissait un véritable regain de popularité. En Grand-Bretagne, ce furent de jeunes artistes, déjà en rapport avec l'école française, qui exploitèrent sérieusement cette technique. William Rothenstein, Charles Conder, Charles Shannon et les disciples de Whistler produisirent tous des oeuvres d'importance à cette époque. The Studio leur apporta son appui mais ils ne connurent pas vraiment de succès commercial. The Neolith les appuya également; cette revue trimestrielle éphémère était fort appréciée et parut en 1907-1908 sous la direction de F. Ernest Jackson et Gerald Spencer-Pryse. Plusieurs artistes contribuèrent à l'illustrer. Kerr-Lawson y envoya des lithographies inspirées de ses panneaux muraux de la cathédrale Saint-Paul et d'Il Colleone.

Lorsque les collaborateurs de la revue se montrèrent intéressés à former une association de lithographes, on organisa une réunion à l'atelier que Kerr-Lawson occupait sur Glebe Place.[65] L'association prit le nom de Senefelder Club, en l'honneur de l'inventeur de la lithographie. Kerr-Lawson, Joseph Pennell, F. E. Jackson et A. S. Hartrick en furent les fondateurs. Ils recrutèrent de nouveaux membres, louèrent un atelier et achetèrent une presse d'occasion pour y imprimer leurs oeuvres. Devenu président, Pennell se mit à organiser des expositions et à écrire livres et articles avec toute l'énergie dont l'homme était capable. La première exposition eut lieu en 1910 et fut suivie de plusieurs autres. Pennell fit connaître le Club internationalement en organisant des expositions non seulement en Grande-Bretagne, mais aussi en Allemagne, en Italie, en Belgique, aux États-Unis, au Canada, en Inde, en Australie et en Nouvelle-Zélande.

Les principales pièces qu'exécuta Kerr-Lawson alors qu'il était membre du Club incluent l'"Ensemble italien", l'"Ensemble espagnol", un ensemble réalisé à partir des panneaux Aldenham et quelques portraits en buste d'amis de Kerr-Lawson. L'"Ensemble italien" (n°s 24-33 du cat.) comportait une série de dix lithographies en couleurs (cinquante impressions chacune) exécutées en 1908 et inspirées des panneaux de Stoke Rochford Hall. L'"Ensemble espagnol" (également connu sous le nom de "Le Gitan espagnol") se composait de six lithographies inspirées de diverses peintures de genre espagnoles. Trois de ses portraits représentaient respectivement Joseph Pennell (n° 39 du cat.), William de Morgan (n° 40 du cat.) et Maurice Hewlett (n° 42 du cat.) Toutes ces lithographies furent bien accueillies par la presse. Citons à ce propos les commentaires de Malcolm Salaman, expert en estampes, qui écrivait en 1919:

Lorsque M. Kerr-Lawson représente un site, il nous le fait connaître à fond; car il a un sens pictural de l'observation qui

---

62. À propos d'Aldenham, voir Dictionary of National Biography, second supplément, vol. II, s.v.

63. Kerr-Lawson fit aussi deux autres sculptures: un buste représentant Caterina (Chelsea Library, London) et l'autre réprésentant Lina Waterfield (British Institute of Florence).

64. Lettre d'Aldenham à Robert J. Lamb, 22 février 1979.

65. Les deux principales sources de renseignements concernant le Club sont A. S. Hartrick, A Painter's Pilgrimage Through Fifty Years, Joseph Pennell, "The Senefelder Club and the Revival of Artistic Lithography," The Studio, février 1914, pp. 3-6.

lui permet d'exprimer, en homme qui maîtrise bien toutes les nuances de la lithographie, aussi bien le détail vivant que l'aspect général des choses.[66]

Un autre expert, Sir Frederick Wedmore, déclarait:

> À propos de la publication par M. Kerr-Lawson d'une série de lithographies en couleurs — L'Ensemble italien — on me rappelle que j'ai déjà mentionné son nom parmi ceux des trois ou quatre hommes au sujet desquels il y avait de bonnes raisons de supposer — et peut-être même de savoir — qu'ils étaient seuls capables d'exécuter des pièces décoratives de grande envergure, des pièces importantes, dignes, valables et tout à fait individuelles ... M. Whistler est probablement le seul autre artiste de notre époque qui ait utilisé la lithogravure pour produire des dessins au lavis de façon aussi significative et aussi réussie que M. Kerr-Lawson.[67]

Grâce aux relations qu'il s'était faites au Senefelder Club, Kerr-Lawson se vit offrir la chance de réaliser des affiches pour le service des transports de Londres. Frank Pick, le président de la compagnie, était réputé pour promouvoir les travaux de haute qualité.[68] D'autres membres du Club, comme Hartrick, Jackson, Pryse et Brangwyn travaillèrent également pour Frank Pick. Les deux compositions de Kerr-Lawson, produites entre 1913 et 1915, étaient destinées à des affiches aux tons de sépia. La première représentait St. Martin-in-the-Fields (n° 58 du cat.) et la seconde l'abbaye de Westminster et l'église St. Margaret. Elles s'inscrivaient dans le cadre d'une campagne visant à encourager le public à redécouvrir Londres qu'il pouvait facilement parcourir en métro. Lorsque les affiches prévues à cet effet firent leur apparition, elles créèrent tout un émoi.[69] À la fin des années 1920, Kerr-Lawson allait réaliser d'autres affiches, cette fois pour le Empire Marketing Board; quelques-unes font partie de cette exposition (n°s 70, 71, 72 du cat.).

En plus d'être un peintre et un lithographe très actif, Kerr-Lawson consacrait aussi une grande partie de son temps à la vente d'oeuvres d'art et à l'expertise de tableaux de maîtres. Ces peintures en vinrent à influencer profondément sa propre oeuvre. Il se spécialisait dans les primitifs italiens du XIVe et du XVe siècles quoique son champ d'action fût beaucoup plus vaste. Il n'était qu'un petit marchand parmi tant d'autres, ce qui ne l'empêchait point de fréquenter des experts tels que Herbert Horne, Roger Fry et Charles Ricketts. Il revendait rarement des ouvrages de grande valeur, mais il lui arrivait parfois de faire une "découverte". Comme pour celles de bien des marchands, ses attributions de tableaux furent quelquefois remises en question.[70] La plupart des ouvrages dont il fit le commerce ne peuvent être ni identifiés, ni retracés. La seule exception d'importance est l'*Adoration des bergers*,

un tableau du Greco, maintenant exposé au Metropolitan Museum of Art de New York. Une copie ancienne du *Couronnement d'épines* de Hieronymous Bosch fait maintenant partie de la collection de son neveu, le Dr J. A. L. McCullough, et une version d'atelier de *La Vierge et l'Enfant Jésus sur un trône*, de Taddeo Gaddi, se trouve maintenant à la Yale University Art Gallery. Kerr-Lawson aurait également eu en mains des ouvrages attribués à Bonifazio da Pitati, à Rembrandt (une collection d'eaux-fortes), au Tintoret, à Boltraffio, à Moroni et à Zoffani. Il agit également comme conseiller artistique auprès de son frère Andrew dont la collection fut donnée au University Art Museum de Berkeley, en Californie. On y trouvait des ouvrages attribués à Ribera, Rembrandt, Hals, Steen, Ostade, Kneller, Lely, Hogarth, Gainsborough, Romney, Constable et Turner.[71]

Son statut d'expert l'amena a rédiger plusieurs articles de revue sur des sujets se rapportant aux arts. Le premier, qui portait sur la peinture en détrempe, parut dans *The Magazine of Art* en septembre 1903. Kerr-Lawson était un auteur agréable qui affectionnait le "beau style" en vogue à son époque et son article, bien que de nature technique, se lit bien.

Le second article publié sous sa signature parut dans le nouveau *Burlington Magazine*. Le sujet était quelque peu limité mais bien élaboré — il s'agissait d'un bref aperçu de l'histoire de l'art anglo-italien au XIXe siècle. Il y traitait de deux portraits — l'un par Watts, l'autre par Alfred Stevens — du Cavaliere William Blundell Spence, personnage anglo-florentin haut en couleurs.

Dans un troisième article écrit pour la même revue, Kerr-Lawson s'attaquait à un sujet plus important. Il essayait de prouver qu'un portrait de Lorenzo Lotto, exposé au Kunsthistorische Museum de Vienne, était en réalité un autoportrait.

Son texte le plus substantiel est un long essai sur "L'Influence de la légende franciscaine sur l'art italien" qui parut en 1908 dans *Assisi of St. Francis,* livre écrit par son amie Clarissa Goff. Comme à l'accoutumée, le texte, bien rédigé, s'appuie sur une connaissance approfondie des ouvrages en question et il jette une lumière nouvelle sur des points particuliers de style et de technique. Après presque soixante-quinze ans, il mérite encore d'être lu même par des professionnels.

En 1912, Kerr-Lawson participa à l'exposition du Canadian Art Club à Toronto et reprit ainsi contact avec le Canada. Après son départ du pays en 1887, il avait cessé d'exposer activement; aussi fut-il bientôt radié de l'Académie royale des arts du Canada. Ses oeuvres

---

66. Malcolm C. Salaman, *Modern Woodcuts and Lithographs,* pp. 123-24.

67. Extrait de la *Pall Mall Gazette* cité par Hector Charlesworth, "Praise for Canadian Painter," *Saturday Night,* 3 octobre 1914, p. 3.

68. À propos de Pick et de son patronage, voir Christian Barman, *The Man Who Built London Transport* et Michael Levey, *London Transport Posters.*

69. Walter Shaw Sparrow, *Advertising and British Art,* p. 134.

70. On en trouve un exemple dans Roger Fry, *The Letters,* vol. 1, pp. 218-19.

71. Francis E. Vaughan, *Andrew C. Lawson,* pp. 221-25.

avaient été présentées occasionnellement lors d'expositions collectives et il avait gardé contact avec sa famille et certains amis, comme Homer Watson. On le connaissait de réputation, bien plus que par ses ouvrages; on le voyait comme l'un des plus célèbres expatriés canadiens: il était celui qui avait dû s'exiler à l'étranger pour réaliser ses idéaux. Lorsque Edmund Morris et Curtis Williamson avaient fondé le Canadian Art Club en 1907, ils avaient entre autres pour objectif d'insuffler une vie nouvelle à la scène artistique en attirant au pays les gens de talent qui l'avaient quitté. Dans son discours inaugural, prononcé lors de la première exposition du Club, le président d'honneur, D. R. Wilkie, avait posé la question suivante:

> Combien de fois avons-nous entendu proclamer que le Canada est une nation sans art! Pour démontrer la fausseté de cette affirmation, nous n'avons qu'à consulter les listes officielles du Salon de France, de la Royal Academy, de l'International Society de Londres, du Royal Institute de Glasgow, de la National Academy de New York et de diverses expositions internationales tenues à travers le monde pour constater qu'il y a des Canadiens qui occupent une position respectée et éminente parmi les grands peintres du monde. Des gens comme Paul Peel, [Sir James Jebusa] Shannon, Blair Bruce, J. Kerr-Lawson, [Frederick C. V.] Ede, Mme Stanhope Forbes et Mary Bell Eastlake ainsi que les sculpteurs [Louis-Philippe] Hébert, [Alfred] Laliberté et [A. Phimister] Proctor, pour ne nommer qu'eux, ont fait honneur à leur pays d'origine tout en accédant personnellement à la notoriété.[72]

Kerr-Lawson était donc tenu en haute estime par ses compatriotes comme en fait foi le bref aperçu de sa carrière qui parut dans *Saturday Night*:

> Plusieurs seront heureux d'apprendre la position éminente qu'a méritée à l'étranger le peintre canadien J. Kerr-Lawson, ancien résident de Toronto qui vit depuis un certain nombre d'années en Angleterre ... M. Kerr-Lawson se consacre à la peinture architecturale et à la lithographie dans sa forme la plus élevée, ce en quoi il s'avère un digne émule de Whistler. Dans cette dernière catégorie, plusieurs de ses ouvrages ont été portés aux nues par la critique de Grande-Bretagne et du continent. Quant à ses peintures à l'huile, elles sont remarquables par leurs superbes coloris et leur facture lisse et fine ... À tous points de vue, ce Torontois est reconnu comme un artiste accompli, au sens le plus plein du mot.[73]

Le président du Club, Homer Watson, invita Kerr-Lawson à exposer sous l'égide de l'association, et, en 1912, lui et W. H. Clapp en furent élus "peintres membres". Selon le critique du *News*, les cinq sujets siciliens exposés en 1912 étaient "de parfaits exemples d'une technique parvenue à maturité". Il ajoutait:

> Il semble que M. Kerr-Lawson ait renoncé à son habitude d'étaler une couche de fond généreuse pour plutôt appliquer franchement une couche fine de couleur pure. D'aucuns ont émis l'idée qu'il aurait récemment modifié son style après avoir réalisé des ouvrages décoratifs de grande envergure. Cela est possible, mais les études qu'il a envoyées ne sont pas dépourvues de qualités picturales. Leur composition est excellente et leur couleur, quoique sans relief, est lumineuse et éthérée.[74]

En 1913, Kerr-Lawson exposa au Club deux tableaux de plus grandes dimensions: *Boston* (n° 51 du cat.) et *Winter in Kent* (dont on ignore la localisation actuelle). Le critique du *Globe* jugea que ces oeuvres avaient été "soigneusement et patiemment faites même si elles étaient quelque peu photographiques".[75] Le jeune Lawren Harris, qui écrivait dans *The Year Book of Canadian Art*, fut beaucoup plus positif. Après avoir analysé l'oeuvre d'Ernest Lawson, de New York, il eut ce commentaire:

> Et il y a l'autre Lawson (J. Kerr) qui habite maintenant Londres en Angleterre. Son "Boston" (au Lincolnshire) dans lequel une veille église à tour carrée domine un paysage marécageux, se signale par un art consommé du dessin et un choix heureux des couleurs. Il est précis et même presque méticuleux. Mais le tableau a de l'étoffe avec sa coloration fine aussi délicate que de l'aquarelle.[76]

En 1915, Kerr-Lawson choisit quinze lithographies parmi celles de ses ensembles italien et espagnol ainsi que de sa série anglaise pour les présenter lors de la dernière exposition du Club. Elles furent peu remarquées quoique Hector Charlesworth, le collaborateur canadien du *Studio*, qualifia ces oeuvres de Kerr-Lawson d'"exquises lithographies, dont la renommée a déjà franchi l'Atlantique."[77] Charlesworth faisait partie du Club sans être artiste, et, critique d'art et rédacteur en chef de *Saturday Night*, il ne manqua pas d'informer le public canadien des activités de Kerr-Lawson après 1914. Avec la poussée d'impérialisme qu'occasionna la guerre, la réputation de Kerr-Lawson atteignit son apogée au Canada.

Le déclenchement des hostilités n'allait guère altérer la vie des Kerr-Lawson. Ils ne pouvaient voyager à l'étranger, mais c'était là leur seule contrainte. Comme la guerre se prolongeait, ils y furent un peu plus impliqués. Caterina travailla comme bénévole au Queen Mary's Hostel for Nurses. En 1916, Kerr-Lawson et d'autres artistes de distinction créèrent des timbres commémoratifs qui devaient être vendus au profit du fonds de la Croix Rouge britannique. Un des modèles dont on le sait l'auteur (n° 61 du cat.), une lithographie intitulée *What I Gave I Have*, représente avec simplicité l'image d'une infirmière britannique en train de panser le bras d'un soldat blessé. Il créa également une lithographie qui servit d'affiche pour le recrutement (n° 60 du cat.).

---

72. "Canadian Art is Given Fresh Stimulus," *Toronto World,* 4 février 1908.

73. Hector Charlesworth, "The Pictures of James Kerr-Lawson," *Saturday Night,* 20 juin 1914, p. 4.

74. "Canadian Art Club's 5th Exhibition," *The News,* non daté.

75. "Fine Pictures at the Canadian Art Club Show," *The Globe,* 10 mai 1913.

76. Lawren Harris, "The Canadian Art Club," dans *The Year Book of Canadian Art 1913,* p. 214.

77. Hector Charlesworth, "Studio Talk: Toronto," *The Studio,* mai 1916, p. 274.

En 1916-1917 Kerr-Lawson se lança dans sa plus importante commande du temps de guerre. Il fut promu major par la Commission des archives militaires de guerre de Lord Beaverbrook et il reçut l'ordre de peindre des tabeaux qui refléteraient l'effort de guerre. Il passa l'été et l'automne en Belgique où il fut cantonné aux "Neuf Ormes", une maison située à Poperinghe, près d'Ypres, et au Saskatoon Club à Arras.[78] C'est là qu'il fit des études préparatoires à ses deux grands tableaux: *Arras, the Dead City* et *The Cloth Hall, Ypres*. Il travailla à l'élaboration de ces tableaux dans son atelier de Glebe Place et, en mars 1918, il pouvait annoncer que l'un d'eux était "maintenant bel et bien en voie d'achèvement."[79] C'est à peu près à cette époque qu'une photographie de lui parut dans *Saturday Night;* on le voyait en uniforme, travaillant à sa toile *Arras* . . . . On l'approcha également pour lui proposer de travailler pour les Britanniques et les Australiens. Si les contacts avec les premiers n'aboutirent pas, par contre il acheva pour les seconds une toile intitulée *Refugees Returning to Cambrai under Protection of an Australian Trooper*. Elle se trouve maintenant à l'Art Gallery of New South Wales de Sydney. Il peignit également le portrait d'un militaire australien, le major J. S. S. Anderson, D.S.O., M.C. Ce tableau, qui était intitulé *The Warrior*, fut exposé un peu partout et finalement offert à la Galerie nationale du Canada après sa mort.

Après la guerre, les deux grandes peintures canadiennes de Kerr-Lawson furent choisies pour faire partie d'un vaste arrangement mural destiné à orner la Chambre du Sénat dans l'édifice nouvellement reconstruit du Parlement à Ottawa. Toutefois, avant d'être installées, ces peintures, ainsi que d'autres tableaux de guerre, furent exposés en 1919 et 1920, à la Royal Academy de Londres, à New York, à Ottawa et à Toronto. Le catalogue qui accompagnait l'exposition prenait un ton arrogant et sévère pour fustiger les crimes des Allemands. Par exemple, le commentaire au sujet d'*Arras* . . . affirmait que:

> Cette peinture nous ouvre les yeux . . . sur l'effroyable dévastation que les Allemands apportèrent sur des centaines de milles de territoire français et belge, ainsi que sur le terrible danger auquel la France et la civilisation sont constamment exposés. L'église dont on aperçoit les ruines au premier plan est la cathédrale d'Arras. Elle porte le nom de St-Vaast, d'après le saint qui consacra sa vie à reconstruire les lieux sacrés détruits par les barbares il y a plus de huit cents ans.[80]

Hector Charlesworth, qui faisait le compte rendu de cette exposition, offrit quant à lui une opinion sinon officielle, du moins plus artistique. "M. Lawson", écrivait-il,

est l'un des peintres dont le nom devrait être associé à ceux de Gerald Moira et George Clausen; ce sont des artistes qui ont nettement réussi à peindre des pièces qui s'harmonisent parfaitement avec un style architectural noble. Jamais encore le sens de la couleur, la perfection du dessin, la merveilleuse transparence du coup de pinceau n'ont été si évidents chez M. Kerr-Lawson que dans ces oeuvres. 'Arras' est peint dans des tons plus discrets que son pendant, 'Ypres' . . ., mais son effet décoratif est des plus nobles. Les coloris d'un gris perle semblent intensifier le sentiment de désolation et le tableau tout entier s'humanise avec la présence de cette femme vêtue de noir qui se dresse, solitaire, parmi les ruines alors que sa silhouette se reflète dans l'eau d'un trou d'obus.[81]

Cependant, les artistes plus jeunes, comme Arthur Lismer, voyaient d'un oeil critique l'aspect académique de ces oeuvres et "l'insensée panoplie de guerre"[82] exploitée, selon eux, dans maintes peintures des Souvenirs de guerre, y compris dans celles de Kerr-Lawson. Tout en faisant l'éloge des oeuvres d'A. Y. Jackson et Fred Varley, de Harold Gilman et D. Y. Cameron, Lismer décrivait *The Cloth Hall, Ypres* comme "une interprétation photographique et journalistique sans relief, absolument dépourvue de toute qualité dramatique, ne possédant ni ampleur ni valeur."[83] Du point de vue du Groupe des Sept, *Ypres* et *Arras* sont certainement des tableaux précis, journalistiques, dépourvus de valeur et académiques. Mais, par rapport à plusieurs autres peintures des Souvenirs de guerre, les tableaux de Kerr-Lawson sont assez particuliers car ils ne se complaisent pas dans "l'insensée panoplie de guerre" ni dans l'étalage des morts et des estropiés des tranchées. Leur composition hardie et leurs couleurs contrastantes en font même des oeuvres dramatiques et, en tant que décorations murales du Sénat, elles ont plus d'effet que les trop grands tableaux de chevalet qui les entourent. Si seulement on avait demandé à Kerr-Lawson de décorer la Chambre dans sa totalité!

Alors que la montée du nationalisme artistique durant les années '20 voyait décliner la réputation de Kerr-Lawson au Canada, il jouissait d'une certaine reconnaissance officielle en Grande-Bretagne. En 1922, Brangwyn et lui organisaient la section britannique de la Biennale de Venise. Même si leur sélection incluait Mark Gertler et C. R. W. Nevinson, elle était, dans l'ensemble, plutôt conservatrice, car on y trouvait des noms comme ceux de George Clausen, Agustus John, William Nicholson et Walter Sickert. Kerr-Lawson connut également le succès mondain. Caterina et lui étaient de fervents amateurs de musique et de théâtre et le duc de Bedford de l'époque leur prêta souvent sa loge au Drury Lane Theatre. James Kerr-Lawson était un ami de la cantatrice Eva Turner; il connaissait Pablo Casals et il peignit un portrait du

78. Caterina, dans une note annexée à un formulaire de renseignements de 1920; dossier des coupures de presse sur Kerr-Lawson; librairie de la Galerie nationale du Canada.

79. Lettre de Kerr-Lawson à Alfred Yockney, 23 mars 1918, Imperial War Museum, Londres.

80. Percy Francis Godenrath, *Lest We Forget*, p. 31.

81. Hector Charlesworth, "Reflections," *Saturday Night*, 18 septembre 1920, p. 2.

82. Arthur Lismer, "The Canadian War Memorials," *The Rebel*, octobre 1919, p. 40.

83. Ibid., p. 41.

violoncelliste anglo-espagnol alors très connu, Agustin Rubio (Ferens Art Gallery, Hull). Caterina et lui fréquentaient les membres les plus intellectuels de l'aristocratie tels le diplomate Lord Lothian et Lord et Lady Desborough.[84]

Mais leur amitié la plus notable et la plus notoire fut de loin celle qu'ils entretinrent avec la reine Mary. La Reine avait rencontré Caterina parce que cette dernière faisait du bénévolat à la maison des infirmières pendant la guerre et Caterina avait utilisé toutes les ressources de son charme pour obtenir son patronage. Il y eut par la suite des visites royales à l'atelier et aux expositions de Kerr-Lawson, des échanges de cadeaux à Noël et une correspondance qui devait s'étaler sur trente ans.[85] Parmi les achats et les cadeaux se trouvaient une vue de Florence (n° 45 du cat.) comprise dans cette exposition, l'"Ensemble italien" de lithographies en couleurs et une grande lithographie de St. Martin-in-the-Fields. La plus intéressante de toutes ces pièces était une minuscule lithographie représentant un homme à canne debout devant une maison (Royal Archives, château de Windsor). Elle fut exécutée en 1924 pour la décoration de la fameuse maison de poupée de la Reine.[86] Sir Edwin Lutyens créa la maison et plusieurs artistes de renom l'ornèrent de modèles réduits de leurs oeuvres.

En 1924, Kerr-Lawson exécuta également deux grandes mosaïques de papier qui lui avaient été commandées pour le Palace of Arts de la British Empire Exhibition à Wembley. L'une représentait l'Annonciation (The Annunciation—n° 65 du cat.) et l'autre l'Adoration des bergers (The Adoration of the Shepherds). Il avait déjà utilisé la technique de la mosaïque de papier dans les panneaux ovales de Stoke Rochford House, mais il étaient employés ici à l'échelle d'une murale pour obtenir un effet décoratif sans relief. La mosaïque de papier est essentiellement une forme de collage mais, si l'absence de relief caractérise ces deux techniques, rien ne ressemble moins au collage cubiste que les deux panneaux de Kerr-Lawson. L'immense arc central qui domine leur composition rappelle sans contredit les tableaux de Fra Angelico et d'autres peintres italiens du XVe siècle.

En 1926 et en 1930, il exposa avec succès à la Beaux Arts Gallery. Ces deux expositions comprenaient principalement des scènes de l'Italie, de l'Espagne et du Maroc et elles furent toutes deux bien accueillies. La plupart des critiques s'attardèrent sur la finesse du dessin, sur l'effet décoratif d'une tonalité sans relief et sur le raffinement de certaines touches aussi délicates que discrètes. Les comptes rendus du *Times* et de l'*Illustrated London News* étaient caractéristiques de l'opinion généralement

émise, à savoir que les oeuvres de Kerr-Lawson portaient le "sceau d'une personnalité intéressante, à la fois alerte et méticuleuse, plus préoccupée d'exprimer une idée avec justesse que de l'imposer à l'attention,"[87] ou qu'elles reflétaient une "personnalité bien distincte, ce qui en faisaient des pièces tout à fait originales mais . . . loin de ces expériences tourmentées et de cette audace aventureuse qui ont chambardé l'art d'aujourd'hui."[88]

Durant les années vingt et trente, Kerr-Lawson travailla de plus en plus comme portraitiste. C'est dans ces oeuvres qu'il manifeste d'une façon très évidente l'historicisme qu'il a puisé dans la Renaissance. Ses portraits d'Andrew Lawson (n° 68 du cat.), de Mme Cawthra (n° 79 du cat.) et de Frank Brangwyn (n° 81 du cat.) en sont des exemples typiques.

Le portrait qu'il fit de Brangwyn est probablement le meilleur de tous ceux que l'on vient de mentionner. La figure et le corps de Brangwyn sont représentés fidèlement quoique la pose et le décor soient décoratifs et symboliques. Comme les modèles des portraits de Botticelli, il tient à la main un médaillon représentant la figure de Kerr-Lawson. Les mots inscrits sur le médaillon et dans le coin inférieur droit du portrait témoignent de la profondeur de leur amitié. La zone de couleur unie qui est placée arbitrairement derrière la tête de Brangwyn pour la mettre davantage en évidence rappelle également les techniques de la Renaissance. Toutefois, l'aspect décoratif du portrait, la fermeté de la composition et la gamme soigneusement restreinte des coloris découlent de la tradition *japoniste* alors très populaire. Brangwyn lui-même était un fervent admirateur de l'art japonais et le paravent posé à l'arrière-plan est un exemple de son goût en la matière. Les grues exotiques du tableau peuvent aussi évoquer les nombreux oiseaux du même genre peints par Brangwyn lui-même, dans ses célèbres panneaux de l'Empire britannique.

Kerr-Lawson n'acheva jamais son dernier grand projet; c'était une série de cinq panneaux muraux destinés au hall de White Lodge, résidence de Hamstead du col. A. R. C. Waite et de l'Hon. Mme Waite. Mme Waite, qui avait hérité de la fortune de l'entreprise d'automobiles Austin, s'était liée d'amitié avec Caterina et elle était devenue la principale protectrice de son mari et son plus ardent collectionneur. Ces panneaux représentaient principalement des scènes du Maroc et des pastiches d'ouvrages plus anciens de Kerr-Lawson. Dans *Fortune* (n° 82 du cat.) et *The Mirage* (Alghanim Collection, Windsor, England), l'effet obtenu est plein de charme. Kerr-Lawson travaillait encore à l'achèvement des autres panneaux lorsqu'il mourut.

84. Une grande partie de la correspondance avec Desborough se trouve dans les archives de la famille Lawson.

85. Une grande partie de la correspondance avec la reine Mary se trouve dans les archives de la famille Lawson.

86. Elizabeth Lambert, "Queen Mary's Doll's House," *Architectural Digest*, décembre 1981, pp. 84-89.

87. "Art Exhibitions: Mr. Kerr-Lawson," *The Times*, 26 janvier 1926, p. 17.

88. "Italy Seen by Scottish Artist of European Repute," *The Illustrated London News*, 13 février 1926, p. 261.

Il mourut le lundi, 1er mai 1939, des suites d'une hémorragie cérébrale. Plusieurs journaux d'Écosse, d'Angleterre et du Canada firent paraître une notice nécrologique à son sujet. Tous insistaient sur le fait que, à cause de sa nature modeste et de son exil volontaire, Kerr-Lawson était moins bien connu qu'il ne le méritait. Le *Times* publia un exemple typique du genre d'hommage qu'on rendit à sa personne:

> Kerr-Lawson était d'un caractère aussi scrupuleusement délicat que son art. Il possédait la modestie authentique de celui qui ne se fait jamais valoir lui-même et n'encourage personne à le faire pour lui car les éloges l'embarrassaient. Il avait de vastes connaissances en peinture, ainsi qu'un jugement pénétrant et lucide, mais il n'avançait une opinion que si on la lui demandait. Il portait le plus vif intérêt aux événements quotidiens et il leur appliquait une pensée fantaisiste qui les éclairait toujours d'une lumière nouvelle, mais qui, la plupart du temps, n'arrivait pas à masquer une sympathie inaltérable pour les pauvres et les opprimés. D'un naturel généreux, bon et doux, il était le moins égoïste des amis, et c'est pourquoi il s'en fit de si nombreux, dans toutes les classes de la société, partout où il était et partout où il allait.[89]

Ses funérailles eurent lieu dans la vieille église de Chelsea, le 4 mai. Eva Turner chanta ses extraits favoris d'*Aïda* et plus de quatre-vingts de ses amis assistèrent à la cérémonie. La dépouille mortelle fut incinérée au cimetière Golders Green.

Caterina vécut encore treize ans. Comme il n'était plus là pour la retenir, elle travailla avec détermination à lui assurer une place dans l'histoire. Elle choisit les meilleures de ses pièces qui restaient pour en faire don à divers musées de Grande-Bretagne et du Canada. Elle en réunit d'autres pour les présenter lors de sept expositions commémoratives tenues dans des galeries publiques et commerciales. En 1940, elle se vit accorder une pension de £100 sur les fonds de la Couronne par égard à sa situation financière aussi bien que pour les services rendus à l'art par son mari. Elle commençait à perdre la vue mais le courage lui faisait rarement défaut et sa correspondance avec des amis beaucoup plus jeunes, comme David Carritt, Adrian Bury et Lina Waterfield, était pleine de vie. Elle mourut finalement à la suite d'une défaillance cardiaque, le 11 juin 1952. Ses funérailles eurent lieu dans l'intimité et elle fut incinérée au cimetière Golders Green le 13 juin.

Après la mort de Caterina, la renommée de Kerr-Lawson s'effaça presque complètement. C'étaient là des temps difficiles pour les artistes victoriens et la plupart des contemporains de Kerr-Lawson eurent également à souffrir de cette évolution dans le jugement de la critique. De nos jours, l'art victorien est beaucoup plus respecté et il y a un regain d'intérêt pour les artistes canadiens d'hier. L'heure est donc venue de refaire, du moins en partie, la réputation de Kerr-Lawson.

Kerr-Lawson est intéressant à plusieurs points de vue. Il a connue une vie passionnante sous bien des rapports et il a fréquenté d'importants milieux artistiques et littéraires. Il a maintenu jusque dans notre siècle la tradition britannique dans la culture canadienne. Il a abordé une grande variété de sujets dans une aussi vaste gamme de techniques · et, ce qui est plus important encore, il a crée un grand nombre d'excellentes oeuvres. Celles-ci se distinguent par la hardiesse dans la composition décorative alliée au raffinement dans le traitement de la lumière, de la tonalité, de la couleur et de l'espace. Ces oeuvres méritent certainement de faire partie de notre héritage artistique canadien.

---

89. "Letter of Tribute," *The Times*, 4 mai 1939, p. 21.

CREDITS

Catalogue design and layout: Kenneth Saltmarche, Victor Batten

French translation: K2 TRANSLATIONS, Kingston, Ontario

Type: Souvenir

Paper: Warren's Cameo Dull 160 basis

Cover: Kromekote 10 pt. coated one side

Colour separations: Artcraft Engravers, London, Ontario

Printing: Curtis Co. Ltd., Windsor, Ontario

PHOTOGRAPHIC CREDITS

Colour Illustrations:

Reproduced by Gracious Permission of Her Majesty The Queen   Cat. no. 45

Art Gallery of Windsor   Cat. no. 3 (Cover)

P. J. Gates, London, England   Cat. no. 34

National Gallery of Canada   Cat. no. 6

Monochrome Illustrations:

Reproduced by Gracious Permission of Her Majesty The Queen   Cat. no. 45

Abbot Tincombe Photographic Services Ltd., Vancouver   Cat. nos. 38, 52, 56, 59

K. Y. Alghanim, Windsor, England   Cat. nos. 73, 77, 82

Andover Photo, Inc., Andover, Massachusetts   Cat. no. 11

Art Gallery of Ontario, Toronto   Cat. nos. 4, 42, 65

Beaverbrook Art Gallery, Fredericton   Cat. no. 10

Kevin Brunelle, Pittsburgh, Pennsylvania   Cat. nos. 8, 23, 43, 44, 51, 54, 55, 58, 67

Canadian War Museum, Ottawa   Figs. 5, 6

Ron Chamberlain, Berkeley, California   Cat. nos. 7, 15, 68

Christie, Manson & Woods Ltd., London   Cat. no. 18, figs. 3, 4

A. C. Cooper Ltd., London   Cat. nos. 19, 20, 21

Ivor Fields Photographic, Oxford   Cat. no. 83

The Fine Art Society Limited, London   Cat. nos. 13, 57

The Fitzwilliam Museum, Cambridge   Cat. no. 14

P. J. Gates, London   Cat. nos. 34, 35, 36

Rocky Ieraci, Windsor, Ontario   Cat. no. 48

The Illustrated London News, London   Cat. no. 81

Kensington and Chelsea Public Libraries, London   Cat. no. 69

Jeffrey M. Lash, White Plains, New York   Cat. nos. 66, 76

National Gallery of Canada   Cat. nos. 2, 9, 24-33, 37, 39, 40, 75, 79, 80

National Portrait Gallery, London   Cat. nos. 17, 41

Squibbs' Studios, Tenby, South Wales   Cat. no. 78

VIDA/Saltmarche, Toronto   Cat. nos. 3, 22

University of Guelph, Office of Educational Practice   Cat. nos. 1, 5, 12, 46, 47, 49, 50, 60, 61, 64, 70, 71, 72, 74

Sydney E. Veronique, Hull, England   Cat. no. 53

Lawson family archives   Title page, figs. 1, 2, 7, tailpiece